BASIC IDIOMS IN ENGLISH

NEW EDITION • BOOK 2

HUBERT H. SETZLER, JR.

DOMINIE PRESS, INC.

Publisher: Raymond Yuen
Project Editor: Ronald E. Feare
Covers and Design: Gary Hamada
Illustrations: Sedonia Champlain
Audio Cassette Recordings: Laetitia Sonami

Published by

Dominie Press, Inc.
5945 Pacific Center Boulevard
San Diego, California 92121 U.S.A.

ISBN 1-56270-099-5
Printed in U.S.A.
1 2 3 4 5 6 7 8 9 A 98 97 96 95 94 93

Preface

This book and its companions, Book 1, Book 3 and Book 4, provide students of English with a selection of the most frequently used idioms in this highly idiomatic language. By studying and practicing these idioms both in context and in isolation, and by using them in relevant activities, students will understand and use standard English more effectively.

The interviews in Books 1, 2, and 3 are based on actual, recorded conversations held with a variety of Americans such as businessmen and women, lawyers, homemakers, doctors, nurses, farmers, and other professional people and their children. The use and definition of each idiom agree with current, accepted usage.

There are five modules in this text: DAILY ACTIVITIES, INFORMATION PLEASE, PROBLEMS AND SOLUTIONS, HUMAN RELATIONSHIPS, and IN THE EVENING. Each module is divided into four lessons. Each lessson presents from twelve to fifteen idioms which are introduced in a dialogue in the form of an interview. Then each idiom is listed with its definition and one or more example sentences. Exercises then follow to help students practice and apply these important idioms in a meaningful context.

Each module is a self-contained learning unit. That is, the students do not have to learn the first module in order to study the second module; the modules are independent. The same is true for the lessons. While each lesson can be studied independently from the others, it is recommended that they be taken in order since there is a systematic progression from *Preparing for the Day* to *Getting Ready for Bed*.

Audio cassette recordings are available containing all dialogues and definitions of all idioms.

Table of Contents

Lesson **1**

Preparing for the Day

Interview

The interviewer is talking to Mary Anderson, a housewife and mother, about her daily life.

Int: What time do you arise, Mary?

Mary: Arise? You mean what time do I **get up**? I **get up** around seven.

Int: What **wakes** you up? Your children?

Mary: Sometimes, but usually it's when the alarm **goes off**.

Int: What time do you set the alarm for?

Mary: Seven o'clock every morning.

Int: Do you **get up** immediately?

Mary: No, I lie there for a few minutes because it takes me a while to **pull myself together.**

Int: Is this your normal routine?

Mary: Oh, yes. **Day in and day out!**

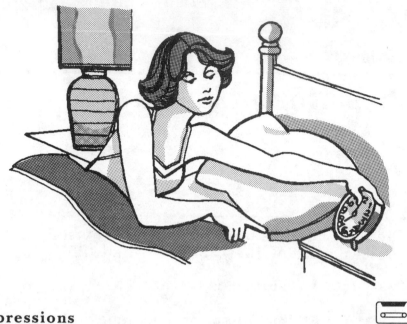

Expressions

---

day in and day out   *daily, every day*
Mary has the same routine at home **day in and day out**.
Day in and day out it rains during the winter months.

get up   *to arise*
Mary usually **gets up** around seven o'clock.
I don't ever **get up** before 10 a.m. on the weekend.

go off   *to ring (said of an alarm clock)*
Mary sets her alarm clock to **go off** at seven every morning.
My alarm didn't **go off** this morning and I overslept.

pull oneself together   *to gain control of oneself*
Before Mary can get up, it takes her a while to **pull** herself **together**.
The child cried for an hour before he **pulled** himself **together**.

wake up   *to awake*
Mary **wakes up** at seven, but she lies in bed a few
minutes before she gets up.
The children always **wake up** before my wife and I
do.

Interview

Mary's husband Ed joins the conversation with the
interviewer.

Int: What do you do when you get up, Mary?
            Do you dress first or have breakfast?

Mary: I usually **put on** my clothes right away.

Ed: Yes, while the children are getting
            dressed, we like to have a cup of coffee
            and **go over** our plans for the day.

Mary: Except for today. This morning was really
            crazy. We **ran out of** cream for the coffee,
            then I burned the toast, and our two-year-
            old son . . .

Ed: Yes, while I was **taking a shower**, our two-
            year-old decided to **give** the cat **a bath** in
            the bathtub!

Expressions

give (someone) a bath   *to bathe someone*
The Anderson's two-year-old son tried to **give** the family cat **a bath**.
The nurse **gave** the newborn baby **a bath** before the evening meal.

go over   *to review*
Mary and Ed enjoy drinking coffee and **going over** their plans for the day.
The girl **went over** yesterday's baseball scores in the newspaper.

put on   *to place on oneself*
                          (clothes, makeup, etc.)
Mary usually **puts on** her clothes as soon as she gets up.
I always **put on** my socks and shoes last, after I eat breakfast.

run out of   *to exhaust one's supply of*
This morning the Andersons **ran out of** cream for their coffee.

Not only has Terry **run out of** money, but she's also **run out of** gas!

take a shower   *to bathe oneself in a shower*
While Ed was **taking a shower**, his son was trying to bathe the cat in the bathtub.
Every morning Mr. Richards **takes a shower** before breakfast.

EXERCISE 1

Select the correct idiom to complete each sentence.

1. Some people prefer to _____ and not bathe in a tub.
   a. give someone a bath
   b. pull oneself together
   c. take a shower
2. What time does your alarm _____ in the morning?
   a. wake up
   b. go off
   c. go over
3. What time do you _____ in the morning?
   a. put on
   b. get up
   c. go over
4. When you _____ money, you cannot pay for your expenses.
   a. run out of
   b. get up
   c. put on
5. When Karen was involved in a bad accident, she had to _____.
   a. day in and day out
   b. pull herself together
   c. go over

EXERCISE 2

Fill in the blanks with the correct idiom. Each idiom
is used only once.

go over	wake up	pull themselves together
goes off	puts on	day in and day out

Most families follow the same routine _____.
They _____ when the alarm clock _____.
The children often get up immediately, but parents
will often lie in bed for a few minutes to _____.
Before breakfast, everyone _____ his or her
clothes and each family member may _____
his or her plans for that day.

Lesson **2**

Transportation

Interview

The interviewer is talking to Helen Fernandez, the head of the data processing department at Berry Cotton Mills.

Int: How do you **get to** work?

Helen: With the high price of gas, I **take the bus** three times a week.

Int: So you drive to work the other two days?

Helen: I usually **share a ride** with my neighbor. This way we can **save on gas**.

Int: Isn't it slow to go by bus?

Helen: Well, a little. Even though the bus **makes good time**, I have to **get ready for** work about twenty minutes earlier.

Int: Have you ever **taken a taxi** to work?

Helen: Yes, once when my car wasn't working and I was too late for the bus. It cost too much money, though!

7

Expressions

get ready for *to prepare oneself or others for*

Helen **gets ready for** work twenty minutes earlier when she takes the bus.
The soccer coach **got** his team **ready for** the important match.

get to *to travel to, to arrive at*

The interviewer asks Helen how she **gets to** work.
If we **get to** the theater early, we can find good seats in the front.

make good time *to travel rapidly and efficiently*

The bus is slower than going by car, but the bus still **makes good time**.
The taxi **made good time** between the airport and downtown during rush hour.

save on gas   *to conserve gasoline*
Helen and her neighbor **save on gas** by driving to
work together.
We can **save on gas** by walking to the store instead of
driving.

share a ride   *to drive with other people*
                              in the same car
Helen and her neighbor **share a ride** to work two
times a week.
Would you like to **share a ride** to the conference?
We can use my car.

take the bus (a taxi)   *to use the bus (a taxi) for*
                              transportation
Helen **takes the bus** to work three times a week.
My car isn't working and I'm late for work, so I have
to **take a taxi** today.

Interview

The interviewer is talking to Helen's son, Jimmy,
about his daily schedule.

     Int: Jimmy, do you take a bus in the morning
          like your mother?

 Jimmy: Yes, she **catches the bus** to work on the
          corner at the end of our block, and I
          catch the bus to school on the next
          corner.

     Int: Does the bus usually get to the corner **on
          time**?

 Jimmy: Almost always. I never have to wait for it
          for more than five minutes.

     Int: Does it **take longer** to go by bus than by
          car?

Jimmy: Well, yes, especially in my case. The bus picks up about forty kids between here and school. I'm the first one to **get on** the bus in the morning and the last one to **get off** the bus in the afternoon.

Expressions

catch the bus   *to board the usual bus*
Jimmy **catches the bus** to school on the next corner.
If I can't **catch the bus** by nine o'clock, I'll have to take a taxi.

get off   *to leave, to descend from*

Jimmy is the last student to **get off** the bus after school.
You **get off** a bus, motorcycle, or airplane, but you **get out** of a car.

get on, get into   *to board, to enter*
Jimmy is the first student to **get on** the bus in the morning.
You **get on** a bus, motorcycle, or airplane, but you **get into** a car.

on time   *exactly at the right time, punctually*
The school bus usually meets Jimmy at the corner **on time**.
The class starts at eight o'clock. Please try to be here **on time**.

take long(er) to   *to require (more) time*
It **takes longer to** travel to school by bus than by car because the bus has to pick up 40 students.
It doesn't **take long to** drive downtown on the weekend.

EXERCISE 1

Select the correct idiom to complete each sentence.

1. I take the express bus to work because it _____.
   a. gets ready for
   b. makes good time
   c. gets on

2. By _____ to work, we save a lot of money each week.
   a. getting off
   b. getting to
   c. sharing a ride

3. Do you know how to _____ the post office from here?
   a. get off
   b. get to
   c. take the bus

4. Peter doesn't want to walk to school today. It
   _____.
   a. gets ready for it
   b. is on time
   c. takes too long

5. Carpooling, or sharing a ride to work allows us to
   _____.
   a. save on gas
   b. catch the bus
   c. take a taxi

EXERCISE 2

Fill in the blanks with the correct idiom. Each idiom is used only once.

get on   get to   catch the bus
on time   get off   makes good time

A: Excuse me. How can I _____ the city zoo from here?

B: You're lucky. You can _____ to the zoo right on this corner. It stops at this corner every fifteen minutes, and it's usually _____.

A: Great. How long is the ride there?

B: About half an hour. It's an express bus, so it _____.

A: How much is the fare?

B: When you first _____the bus, you'll have to pay one dollar.

A: Does the bus stop near the zoo?

B: Yes, it does. You'll _____ on Madison Avenue in front of the zoo.

A: Thanks a lot!

Lesson **3**

At Work, at School

Interview

The interviewer is talking to Rachael Lake, an insurance agent who has risen quickly within her company, City Life Insurance.

Int: Rachael, what are your responsibilities as district manager of City Life?

Rachael: I **am in charge of** sales for the whole district. I **make sure** that all of the new insurance policies are **in order**.

Int: That sounds like a lot of responsibility.

Rachael: It is. I also **keep track of** the activities of all the sales agents. Sometimes they don't **pay attention** to deadlines.

Int: Can this cause problems for you?

Rachael: It sure can. For example, some have problems **turning in** their paperwork. We need the information **in time** to prepare the weekly policy reports.

Int: You must be very busy.

Rachael: Yes, I am. I work so hard during the week that I never **feel like** doing anything on the weekends.

Expressions

be in charge of   *to be responsible for*
Rachael is **in charge of** insurance sales for an entire company district.
Mike is **in charge of** entertainment for the party and I'm in charge of food.

feel like   *to have a desire to*
Rachael doesn't **feel like** doing much on the weekend after a hard workweek.
If you don't **feel like** going out to dinner, it's fine with me.

in order   *arranged appropriately, done correctly*
Rachael's insurance company expects all new policies to be **in order**.

You should check your homework to see that everything is **in order**.

in time   *before the required time*
The agents must return their paperwork **in time** to prepare the weekly reports.
The motorist was able to stop her car **in time** to avoid a serious accident.

keep track of   *to keep a record of,*
                               to know the location of
Rachael **keeps track of** the activities of the insurance agents in her district.
I can't seem to **keep track of** my house and car keys. I often forget where they are.

make sure   *to be sure, to ascertain*
One of Rachael's responsibilities is to **make sure** that the new policies are prepared properly.
The office supervisor has to **make sure** that all the reports are done on time.

pay attention to   *to listen carefully to,*
                               to concentrate on
Some of the insurance agents don't **pay attention to** the work deadlines.
The best students **pay attention to** what their teachers say and to what the homework is.

turn in   *to submit or deliver*
                               something that is due
Some agents forget to **turn in** their work by the deadlines set by the company.
All students should **turn** their assignments **in** before the end of class.

Interview

The interviewer is now talking to Rachael's sister, Heather, about her studies in school.

Int: Well, Heather, school must be easy for you compared to the job your sister has.

Heather: No, it isn't. School is a full-time job. This week I have three term papers to turn in, and I have to make sure that I do my homework **right away**.

Int: But you don't have the pressure that your sister has.

Heather: That's not true. I have to pay close attention to what my professors say. Sometimes I have to study all night just to **keep up with** my courses.

Int: Is that right? I thought that you were in school only four hours a day.

Heather: Well, yes, but after class I have to study for two or three more hours. I feel like I can't **take time off** for anything. Rachael, **on the other hand**, has a flexible schedule. She can **keep her own hours.**

Rachael: That's not really true. I have to **put up with** many problems too. I often bring work home with me. Just **keeping up with** the paperwork seems like a full-time job!

Expressions

keep one's own hours *to arrange one's own work schedule*
Rachael has some flexibility in **keeping her own hours** at work.
People who run a business at home **keep their own hours**.

keep up with *to maintain the necessary speed or rate for*
Heather has trouble **keeping up with** the work in all of her courses.
Rachael finds that **keeping up with** the office paperwork is a full-time job too.

on the other hand *however, in contrast*
Heather has a fixed schedule. **On the other hand**, Rachael has a more flexible one.
I'd like to attend school for another term. **On the other hand**, I could make money if I worked instead.

put up with *to tolerate, to stand*
Both Rachael and Heather have to **put up with** many problems and difficulties.
I can't **put up with** noise while I'm trying to study.

right away *immediately, without delay*
Heather has to make sure that she does her homework **right away**. If she doesn't, then she can't keep up with the work.
The office manager wanted several employees to come to her office **right away**.

take time off *to arrange to be free from work*
Heather never seems to be able to **take time off** from her studies.
Todd has been working so hard for several weeks that he's ready to **take some time off** for a short vacation.

EXERCISE 1

Select the correct idiom to complete each sentence.

1. Would you please _____ that these projects are
   finished today?
   a. make sure
   b. turn in
   c. feel like

2. The teacher told the students to _____ several
   important sections of the text.
   a. put up with
   b. pay attention to
   c. keep up with

3. There's no hurry to complete this work. Do it
   whenever you _____ it.
   a. take time off
   b. keep your own hours
   c. feel like

4. The students who enrolled in the class late can't
   _____ the other students.
   a. be in charge of
   b. keep up with
   c. keep track of

5. My boss was upset because I didn't turn in the
   reports _____ to meet the deadline.
   a. in time
   b. on the other hand
   c. in or

EXERCISE 2

Fill in the blanks with the correct idiom. Each idiom is used only once.

feel like   in order   is in charge of
keep track of   put up with   turn in
right away   on the other hand
take some time off

Bob Sampson is a supervisor in the sales department.
He ①_____ five employees. He has to
②_____ their work, and to make sure that
all their work is ③_____.

This morning Bob Samson is a little sick; he doesn't
④_____ going to the office. He knows
that he can ⑤_____ if he wants to.
⑥_____, he also knows that there is a lot of
work waiting on his desk.

Suddenly the phone rings. His boss wants him to
come to the office ⑦_____. One of Bob's
employees forgot to ⑧_____ an important
report, and the boss is angry. The boss cannot
⑨_____ serious mistakes like that!

Lesson **4**

Shopping

Interview

The interview is talking to Carol Schmidt, a salesperson in a small department store, about the types of shoppers that come in her store.

Int: I suppose that shoppers have changed a great deal **over the years**.

Carol: Actually, shoppers are basically the same. People still **try on** all the new clothes. They **try out** all the new items like sports and exercise equipment.

Int: Are there any items that are very popular now?

Carol: Shoppers really **go for** the new electronic equipment. Video games are particularly popular.

Int: Do shoppers generally **pick out** the less expensive items?

Carol: Not necessarily, but value for the money is very important these days.

Expressions

go for   *to be attracted to*
Shoppers really **go for** the new electronic gadgets.
Jill really **goes for** Ed because he's such an
interesting person.

over the years   *throughout a period of years*
The habits of shoppers have not changed very much
over the years.
Over the years, electronic equipment has become
more sophisticated.

pick out   *to choose, to select*
Typical shoppers take several minutes to **pick out**
what they want.
Would you help me **pick out** a nice birthday card to
send to my sister?

try on   *to check clothes by wearing*
People are most interested in **trying on** the newest
clothing fashions.
Try on this shirt before you make up your mind.

try out   *to check the function of, to test*
Some shoppers like to **try out** new equipment such
as sporting goods.
Before I buy that car, I want to **try** it **out** for an hour
or so.

Interview

The interviewer continues his discussion with Mrs.
Schmidt.

     Int: Are there many **bargain hunters** today?

     Carol: At today's prices? Of course! Typical
              shoppers will come in and pick out what
              they want. They may take several minutes
              to **think** it **over**. Then they will **make up**
              their minds to buy the item. A minute
              later, they may **change their minds** and
              put the item **back**.

     Int: Does that kind of shopper upset you?

     Carol: On, no! **On the whole**, I would rather see
              consumers **get the most for** their money.
              I'm a bargain hunter myself!

Expressions

bargain hunter   *someone who seeks value*
                            at a low cost
Carol still sees a lot of **bargain hunter**s in her store.
With rising inflation and a high cost of living, more
people become **bargain hunters**.

change one's mind   *to alter a decision or opinion*
Some shoppers **change their minds** about buying a
store item.
I wanted to buy the red sweater, but I **changed my**
mind and bought a blue one.

get the most for   *to obtain the maximum value or quality*

Consumers are trying to **get the most for** their money.

I'll try to **get the most for** my car when I sell it.

make up one's mind   *to finally decide*

Some shoppers **make up their minds** to buy an item after several minutes of thinking.

My wife helped me to **make up my mind** about the color of my new suit.

on the whole   *generally, in general*

On the whole, the shoppers in Carol's store are happy with their purchases.

I'm glad to say that, **on the whole**, my life is easier than it was before.

put back   *to replace, to return*

Some shoppers decide to **put back** an item that they want to buy.

I **put** the book **back** on the shelf because it didn't seem interesting.

think over   *to carefully consider*

If items are expensive, shoppers will **think over** their decisions carefully.

Don't change your mind so quickly. **Think** it **over** first!

EXERCISE 1

Select the correct idiom to complete each sentence.

1. Our company has had a couple of short periods
   of low sales, but _____, it's been a very good year.
   a. over the years
   b. on the whole
   c. changing my mind

2. First _____ several suits, and then you can decide.
   a. try out
   b. try on
   c. put back

3. I can't decide between these two cars. Of course
   I want to _____ my money.
   a. get the most for
   b. try out
   c. make up my mind

25

4. I used to spend money carelessly, but _____, I have become a bargain hunter.
   a. over the years
   b. picking out
   c. putting it back

5. I'll come back tomorrow and let you know my decision. I want to _____ first.
   a. change my mind
   b. pick it out
   c. think it over

EXERCISE 2

Fill in the blanks with the correct idiom. Each idiom is used only once.

make up my mind	put . . . back	tried . . . on
got the most for	bargain hunter	picked out
changed your mind	think . . over	went for

A: Have you seen my car keys? I put them on the counter when I returned.

B: Yes, I _____ your keys _____ in the hall drawer. Did you have fun shopping?

A: Oh, yes, I bought a new coat. Here, isn't it nice?

B: I can see how you _____ it. It's beautiful. Is it expensive?

A: Yes, it is, but it's good quality. I'm sure that I _____ my money.

A: I _____ several coats and I _____ all of them _____. However, I was able to _____ quickly about this one.

B: Didn't you _____ it _____ first? You might have _____ because of the price.

A: I'm not a _____ like you. I deserve expensive things!

Module 1 Review

EXERCISE 1

Select the correct idiom for the boldface phrase or word.

1. Do you know who **is responsible for** arrangements for the tournament?
   a. is in charge of
   b. is keeping up with
   c. feels like

2. Marsha **arises** in the morning at the same time every day.
   a. gets to
   b. gets up
   c. gets ready

3. If you **alter your decision** one more time, I'll stop helping you.
   a. make up your mind
   b. pull yourself together
   c. change your mind

4. **Daily** Tanya tries to control her eating, but she hasn't been able to lose weight.
   a. over the years
   b. on the whole
   c. day in and day out

5. We thought we knew how to **travel to** the theater, but instead we got lost.
   a. get on
   b. get to
   c. go for

6. The supervisor had to remind an employee to
    come to work **punctually**.
    a. on time
    b. in time
    c. right away

7. Did Max **submit** our committee recommendations
    to the right person?
    a. turn in
    b. put up with
    c. keep up with

8. Sarah is not a very orderly person; **however**, she
    has a great memory.
    a. on the other hand
    b. on the whole
    c. in order

9. I can't believe that we **exhausted our supply of**
    milk already.
    a. went over
    b. saved on
    c. ran out of

10. James insisted on **testing** the golf clubs before he
    bought them.
    a. trying on
    b. trying out
    c. picking out

EXERCISE 2

**Write a short story for each picture by using the suggested
idioms. You may use other idioms as well. The first one is
done for you.**

1. (left picture, page 11)
    keep one's own hours, take time off, get off,
    take the bus, save on gas

This morning Charlie and his father felt like going to the park. His father keeps his own hours, so he took some time off from work. Right now Charlie and his father are getting off the bus. They took the bus to the park to save on gas.

2. (right picture, page 11)
   share a ride, make good time, get to, on time,
   pay attention to

   _____
   _____
   _____
   _____
   _____
   _____

3. (picture, page 22)
   pick out, put on, make sure, on the whole,
   make up one's mind

   _____
   _____
   _____
   _____
   _____
   _____

4. (picture, page 25)
   bargain hunter, try out, think it over,
   change one's mind, day in and day out

   _____
   _____
   _____
   _____
   _____
   _____

Lesson **1**

On The Telephone

Interview

The interviewer is talking by telephone to the receptionist at Wong Office Supplies. He needs to talk to the company president, Larry Wong.

Receptionist:	Good morning. Wong Office Supplies. May I help you?
Int:	Good morning. This is Mr. Setzler. I'm trying to **get in touch with** Mr. Larry Wong.
Receptionist:	I'm sorry, but Mr. Wong **is tied up** on another telephone line right now. May I have him **call** you **back**?
Int:	Well, could you **put me on hold** for a while?
Receptionist:	Yes, certainly. As soon as he **is free**, I'll **put** you **through** to him.
Int:	Thank you.

Expressions

be free   *to be available*

The interviewer can talk to Mr. Wong as soon as he **is free.**

If you**'re free** tonight, would you like to go to the movies?

be tied up   *to be occupied, to be busy*

When the interviewer calls, Mr. Wong is **tied up** on another telephone line.

Unfortunately, Frank is **tied up** this afternoon and can't come to the meeting.

call back   *to return a telephone call*

Mr. Wong can **call** the interviewer **back** when he is finished on the other line.

Would you **call** me **back** as soon as you've eaten dinner?

get in touch with   *to contact, to reach*

The interviewer is trying to **get in touch with** Mr. Wong.

Barbara said that she'd **get in touch with** me, but she hasn't called or written.

put on hold   *to make someone wait on the telephone*

The receptionist will **put** the interviewer **on hold** for a short while.

The secretary **put** me **on hold** while she looked for the information I needed.

put through (to)   *to connect (to someone) by telephone*

The receptionist will **put** the interviewer **through** to Mr. Wong soon.

Could you please **put** me **through** to the credit department!

Interview

The interviewer is now talking to Larry Wong, president of the company.

Larry: Good morning. What can I do for you?

Int: I'm calling about the telephone survey I'm conducting. Remember? I want to know how often each day you **make a call**.

Larry: Of course. Let me see . . .I think I make about twenty calls a day. My secretary knows exactly. I have . . . Excuse me. There's someone on the other line. Let me **put** you **in touch with** my secretary.

Int: **Never mind**, Mr. Wong. I have most of what I need.

Larry: Fine. You can always **drop me a line** to request further information.

Int: That's a kind offer. You may **hear from** me again.

Expressions

drop a line   *to send a note or letter*
If the interviewer needs more information, he can
drop Mr. Wong **a line**.
Matthew **dropped** me **a line** during his trip to Mexico.

hear from   *to receive news by*
                       telephone or mail
It is possible that Mr. Wong will **hear from** the
interviewer again.
Have you **heard from** your friend in Spain recently?

make a call   *to telephone,*
                        to use the telephone
The interviewer wants to know how often each day
Mr. Wong **makes a call**.
Excuse me. May I use your telephone? I have to
make a call.

never mind   *it isn't necessary,*
                       don't concern yourself
The interviewer responds, "**Never mind**", when Mr.
Wong wants to connect him to the secretary.
Can't you help me? **Never mind**. I'll do it myself.

put in touch with   *to connect to*
The interviewer doesn't need to be **put** in **touch with**
the secretary.
The company operator **put** me **in touch** with the
head of the department.

EXERCISE 1

Select the correct idiom to complete each sentence.

1. I'll have to _____ while I answer the other telephone in the office.
   a. drop you a line
   b. hear from you
   c. put you on hold

2. Pat was lucky that so many of her friends _____ to help her move.
   a. were free
   b. were tied up
   c. put her in touch

3. For further information, I'll have to _____ the customer service department.
   a. call you back
   b. put you through
   c. put in touch

4. Be sure to _____ during your trip to Europe.
   a. hear from me
   b. drop me a line
   c. tie me up

5. Sam had to stay late at the office, so he _____ to his wife.
   a. got in touch
   b. never mind
   c. made a call

EXERCISE 2

Fill in the blanks with the correct idiom. Each idiom is used only once.

call . . . back   get in touch with   are free
never mind   am tied up   hear from
make a call

A: Jake, I wonder if you _____ to help me a moment.

B: I'm sorry, right now I _____ with this chore. I can help you in a few minutes, though.

A: Oh, _____. I think I can do it alone.

B: Did you ever _____ Mike about the party?

A: Oh, no, I didn't. He was supposed to _____ me, but he didn't.

B: That's just like Mike. Why don't you _____ him _____ now?

A: I'll _____ to him in a moment. I'm busy trying to fix this light!

Information, Please MODULE 2

Lesson 2

The Library

Interview

The interviewer is talking to Emily Neal, head librarian of the Community Library.

Int: Good morning, Mrs. Neal. Oh, I see you're busy. I'll come back later.

Mrs. Neal: No, no. I'm glad you **came in** now. I've been able to **put together** most of the information you wanted. Here it is.

Int: Thanks very much.

Mrs. Neal: There is one problem. As I **looked over** your questions, I **ran across** one that I couldn't **make out**.

Int: Which one was that?

Mrs. Neal: It **had** something **to do with** people in the library.

Int: Yes, I wanted to know what kinds of people use the library.

Mrs. Neal: Oh, all kinds of people. At lunchtime, adults come in to look at the newspapers and periodicals. After school, students come in to **look up** information for their school assignments.

Int: I see.

Expressions

come in   *to enter*
Mrs. Neal is glad that the interviewer **came in** the library to see her.
Won't you **come in** for a while and have a cup of coffee?

have to do with   *to pertain to, to concern*
Mrs. Neal didn't understand one of the interviewer's questions that **had to do with** people in the library.
I believe that her job **has to do with** Customs Import Laws.

look over   *to review, to examine*
Mrs. Neal **looked over** the interviewer's questions
very carefully in order to collect the necessary
information.
Ted always **looks** his homework **over** before he turns
it in to his teacher.

look up   *to search for,*
                                 to locate information about
Students come in the library after school to **look up**
information.
You can **look** her address **up** in the telephone book.
I think it's listed.

make out   *to understand, to identify*
Mrs. Neal couldn't **make out** one of the interviewer's
questions.
It was so dark that Carol couldn't **make** anything **out**.

put together   *to asemble, to gather*
Mrs. Neal was able to **put together** the information
that the interviewer needed.
My mother helped me to **put** the kite **together** the
right way.

run across   *to find unexpectedly*
Mrs. Neal was surprised to **run across** a question that
she couldn't understand.
Mother **ran across** some old family photographs
while she was cleaning out a closet.

Interview

The interviewer is continuing his conversation with Mrs. Neal.

> **Mrs. Neal:** **By the way**, do you have a library card?
>
> **Int:** No, I'm sorry, I don't have one. What do I have to **go through** to get one?
>
> **Mrs. Neal:** It's no problem. Here's the form. You **fill in** your name, address, and telephone number on this side. You can **read over** the library rules on the back of the form.
>
> **Int:** Should I **fill** it **out** now?
>
> **Mrs. Neal:** No, you can take it home and return it any time.
>
> **Int:** Thank you, Mrs. Neal. You've been a big help.

Expressions

by the way   *incidentally*
The librarian asks, "Do you have a library card, **by the way?**"
By the way, I'm having a little party tonight. Can you come?

read over   *to read quickly, to scan*
The interviewer should **read over** the library rules on the back of the form.
Here are the agenda items for the meeting. I'd like you to **read** them **over** before we start.

fill in   *to complete,*
                          to write answers in (blanks)
The interviewer has to **fill in** several blanks on the library form.

In the exercise section of each lesson in this book, you have to **fill** the blanks **in** with the correct forms of the idioms.

fill out   *to complete (forms,*
                                   applications, etc.)
The interviewer doesn't have to **fill out** the form right away; he can do it later at home and then bring it back.
You'll have to **fill** three applications **out**, one for each of the three job openings you're interested in.

go through   *to experience, to endure*
The interviewer asked what he had to **go through** to get a library card.
Most parents **go through** a lot of pain and effort to raise their children well.

EXERCISE 1

Select the correct idiom to complete each sentence.

1. The owners _____ a new management team to run company operations after the previous managers were fired for incompetence.
   a. made out
   b. brought back
   c. put together
2. When you take books out of the library, don't forget to _____.
   a. fill them out
   b. bring them back
   c. look them up
3. I didn't expect all of this office paperwork. What does it _____ my job?
   a. run across
   b. have to do with
   c. look over

4. Successful teachers _____ a lot of work to educate their students well.
   a. make out
   b. come in
   c. go through

5. Before you sign this important contract, you should _____ carefully.
   a. read it over
   b. run it across
   c. look it up

EXERCISE 2

Fill in the blanks with the correct idiom. Each idiom is used only once.

by the way	filled out	come in
look up	had to do with	fill in
putting together	went through	looked over

George went to the library to _____ some information for a class assignment. The assignment _____ the historical causes of the American Civil War. He didn't have a library card, so he _____ a form at the front desk. There were only a few blanks that he had to _____.
The library assistant _____ the form when George completed it. Everything was in order, so George got a temporary card.

George had some trouble _____ the necessary information for his term paper, so he asked a librarian for assistance. The librarian _____ a lot of effort to help George find the information he needed. Afterwards George thanked her, and she said that he could _____ any time for help. _____, George received an "A" on the paper.

Lesson **3**

Directions (Travel)

Interview

The interview is walking on city streets and is lost. He has stopped a businessman on the street and is talking to him.

Int: Excuse me, sir. I'm lost. Can you tell me how to get to the Yates Building? I've been looking **all over** for it.

Man: I'll **do my best**. Let's see . . .**First of all**, the Yates Building is on Fifth Street, so you'd better **turn around**.

Int: I didn't realize that I was going the wrong way!

Man: Yes, you were. **Go up to** that corner in the distance, where the bus is turning right. You turn left and eventually you'll **come to** a big hill.

Man: The Yates Building is at the top of the hill, right?

Int: Exactly. You can't miss it.

43

Expressions

all over   *everywhere*
The interviewer has been looking **all over** for the Yates Building.
The child searched **all over** the house for her lost doll.

come to   *to reach, to arrive at*

The interviewer will be near the Yates Building when he **comes to** a big hill.
Walk down this street until you **come to** a small park and then turn right.

do one's best   *to use one's maximum ability*
The businessman will **do his best** to give the right directions.
If you **do your best** in school, you'll undoubtedly succeed.

44

first of all   *to begin with, to start with*
First of all, the interviewer has to turn and walk the
opposite direction.
We'll discuss business **first of all**, then we'll eat
lunch, and finally we'll play a round of golf.

go up to   *to approach, to get close to*
The interviewer has to **go up to** a street corner in
the distance.
The student hesitated to **go up to** the teacher and
ask for help.

turn around   *to turn and face the opposite way*
The interviewer has to **turn around** and go the
opposite way.
Turn around and look in the mirror behind you.

Interview

The interviewer is continuing his conversation with
the businessman.

> **Int:**   I don't have my watch today. What time is
>   it?
>
> **Man:**   It's almost one o'clock.
>
> **Int:**   My goodness. I **had better** hurry or I
>   won't **get back** to work on time. I just
>   started working at the Yates Building last
>   week. I wouldn't want to **show up** late so
>   soon.
>
> **Man:**   I see. Well, the Yates Building is too **far
>   away** for you to get back before one
>   o'clock. Why don't you catch the bus?
>
> **Int:**   Oh, does the bus pass by here?

Man: Yes, it should come by **before long**. Look, there it is.

Int: Great. I really appreciate your help!

Expressions

---

before long   *soon, after a short period of time*
A bus that passes the Yates Building should come by **before long**.
Before long I need to buy some new tires for my car.

had better   *should, ought to*
The interviewer **had better** hurry or he'll be late returning to work.
You **had better** wear a raincoat outside. It's raining rather hard.

far away   *at a great distance*
The interviewer didn't realize that the Yates building was too **far away** to walk there within a few minutes.
With a telescope, it is possible to look **far away** into space.

get back   *to return*
The interviewer has to **get back** to work after the lunch hour.
Joyce usually **gets back** home from school at around 5 o'clock every day.

show up   *to appear, to arrive*
The interviewer doesn't want to **show up** late to work because he just started working on a new job.
We had to wait over an hour before Joe **showed up**. We were rather upset at him.

EXERCISE 1

Select the correct idiom to complete each sentence.

1. If you want to drive east, you should _____; you're going west right now.
   a. come to
   b. turn around
   c. get back

2. I thought that the work would take several hours, but I was done _____.
   a. before long
   b. first of all
   c. all over

3. In a bank, people wait in line before they can _____ a counter.
   a. show up
   b. go up to
   c. do their best

4. Irene searched _____ the house for her keys, but she couldn't find them.
   a. far away
   b. had better
   c. all over

5. If Steve doesn't _____ soon, we should leave without him.
   a. show up
   b. had better
   c. come to

EXERCISE 2

Fill in the blanks with the correct idiom. Each idiom is used only once.

before long	shows up	first of all
far away	had better	getting back

A: What are our plans for today?

B: _____, we're going to walk around the shopping center, then we're having dinner in Old Town, and finally we're seeing a movie.

A: Isn't the movie theater _____ from Old Town?

B: No, there's a new theater that's closer. We're going there.

A: Even so, that's a lot to do in one afternoon. We _____ leave soon.

B: We can't leave before Tina _____. She's late.

A: She's always a little late. I'm sure that she'll arrive _____.

B: I hope so. I don't like _____ home too late!

Lesson **4**

Requests For Directions

Interview

The interviewer is talking to Kay Durham, a supervisor at Data Electronics, who is helping a new employee, Bill Wheat, to operate a duplicating machine.

Int: Do you always have to teach new employees to run the machines, Kay?

Kay: Usually not. Occasionally I do, however. This is our new model, and I am the only one in the office trained to operate it.

Bill: Well, I give up. I've tried it **again and again**, I can't **get it right**.

Kay: Okay, Bill, tell me how you're using it.

Bill: Well, I **turn on** the machine like this. Then I put in the pages like this, **one after another**. See, the copies are unclear.

Kay: I see. This is a problem I'll have to fix after lunch. **Turn off** the power for now.

Bill: How do you **turn** it **off**?

49

Expressions

again and again   *repeatedly*
Bill has tried **again and again** to operate the
duplicating machine properly.
Again and again I called the office number, but there
was never an answer.

get it right   *to do properly, to succeed*
Bill is ready to give up on the copy machine because
he can't **get it right**.
The little boy practiced riding his new bicycle until
he **got it right**.

one after another   *in sequence, in a series*
The pages go into the duplicating machine **one after
another**.
One after another the sick patients in the waiting
room saw the doctor.

turn off   *to disconnect, to terminate*
Bill **turns off** the power to the machine because it
isn't working properly.
Could you please **turn** the lights **off** when you leave
the room?

turn on   *to start, to connect*
Bill knows how to **turn on** the machine and put the
pages into it.
I'd like to see the nightly news. Could you **turn** the
TV **on**?

Interview

The interviewer is talking to Bill at the duplicating machine later in the day.

Int: Well, Bill, did Kay **find out** what the problem was?

Bill: Yes, she did. The copies are clear now.

Int: After **working on** this machine all day, are you finally **getting the hang of** it?

Bill: **To my surprise**, it's not so difficult. It becomes much easier **after a while**.

Int: Kay must have **clued** you **in** well.

Bill: Yes, she did. Before long, I'll really be good at it, too!

Expressions

after a while   *later, after a short period of time*

Operating the office machine is easier for Bill **after a while**.
After a while, you'll feel more comfortable speaking English.

clue in   *to give information to, to advise*

Kay **clued** Bill **in** well on how to operate the duplicating machine.
I asked Margaret to **clue** me **in** on what happened at the meeting that I missed yesterday.

find out   *to discover, to learn*
Kay was able to **find out** what the problem was with
the duplicating machine and to fix it.
William tried to **find out** why he got a "B" on his test
instead of an "A".

get the hang of   *to do properly,*
                                 to succeed (to get it right)
After enough practice on the office machine, Bill
has **gotten the hang of** it.
It's difficult to **get the hang of** skiing, but the effort
is worthwhile.

to one's surprise   *surprisingly, unexpectedly*
To Bill's surprise, it didn't take long to get the hang
of operating the copier.
The little boy got the hang of riding his bicycle in
only one day, **to everyone's surprise**.

work on   *to operate, to attempt;*
                                to fix or complete
Bill must have a big project; he's been **working on**
the duplicating machine all day.
Kay is the only one in her office that is trained to
work on the duplicating machine.
How long have you been **working on** that
assignment?

EXERCISE 1

Select the correct idiom to complete each sentence.

1. It's too hot in this room. Could you _____ the air conditioning?
   a. clue in
   b. turn on
   c. after a while

2. This video game is too confusing. I can't _____ playing it.
   a. find out
   b. turn off
   c. get the hang of

3. After forming a line, the children entered their classroom _____.
   a. again and again
   b. one after another
   c. to turn off

4. Could you _____ on what happened at the meeting yesterday?
   a. clue me in
   b. find me out
   c. get it right

5. _____ my parents suddenly stopped by one day early in the morning.
   a. again and again
   b. after a while
   c. to my surprise

EXERCISE 2

Fill in the blanks with the correct idiom. Each idiom is used only once.

to their surprise	worked on	after a while
turned on	get the hang of	find out
clued in	again and again	

Bobby and Michael _____ their school assignments all Saturday morning. In the afternoon, they _____ Bobby's computer and started playing a new video game that Bobby just bought. Bobby already knew how to play, but Michael had to be _____ on the rules.

In the beginning the game was difficult for them, but _____ they were able to _____ it. They played the game _____ all afternoon. However, _____, they were never able to _____ how to win the game.

Module 2 Review

EXERCISE 1

Select the correct idiom for the boldface phrase or word.

1. Mrs. Larsen **is occupied** in a conference and is not available at this time.
   a. put on hold
   b. tied up
   c. all over

2. Operator, could you please **connect me** to the information booth?
   a. put me through to
   b. bring me back to
   c. clue me in on

3. I really appreciated it when Mark **sent me a note** during his trip.
   a. called me back
   b. put me in touch with
   c. dropped me a line

4. We couldn't figure out how the lecture **pertained to** the course material.
   a. had to do with
   b. filled in
   c. made out

5. The research librarian can help you **locate** the information you need.
   a. work on
   b. go through
   c. look up

6. Luke hesitated to **approach** the girl he liked and to ask for a date.
   a. come to
   b. go up to
   c. run across

7. I put on roller skates for the first time and **soon** I was skating well.
   a. before long
   b. first of all
   c. by the way

8. Do you have any idea whether Don's going to **appear** at the party tonight?
   a. get back
   b. show up
   c. come in

9. Jane couldn't **understand** the message in the handwritten letter.
   a. get it right
   b. look over
   c. make out

10. I tried to **discover** how old he was, but he wouldn't reveal his age.
    a. find out
    b. come to
    c. hear from

EXERCISE 2

Write a short story for each picture by using the suggested idioms. You may use other idioms as well.

1. (left picture on page 54)
   look over, turn on, turn off, again and again

_____
_____
_____
_____
_____
_____

2. (middle left picture, page 54)
    do one's best, before long, get it right,
    one after another

_____
_____
_____
_____
_____

3. (middle right picture, page 54)
    be tied up, work on, first of all, go through

_____
_____
_____
_____

4. (right picture, page 54)
    to his surprise, go up to, bring back, after a while

_____
_____
_____
_____
_____

Lesson 1

Asking for Help

Interview

The interviewer (Hugh) is talking with Pete Martin, a fireman, when one of Pete's neighbors, Mrs. Vega, comes running up to them.

Pete:	Uh-oh, Hugh. I'm in for trouble again.
Mrs. Vega:	Pete! I'm so glad you're home! Could you **give me a hand**? My kitten Snowy is up a tree and can't get down.
Pete:	I'd be glad to **lend a hand. Just a minute** and I'll get my ladder.
Mrs. Vega:	It's so nice of you to help.
Pete:	Come on, Hugh. You can **pitch in**, too.
Int:	Okay. What should I do?
Pete:	You can hold the ladder for me. Snowy is really way up there, almost to the top.
Int:	Shouldn't I climb up with you?

58

Pete: No, I'm **used to** high places. You
might fall and kill yourself.

Int: I wouldn't want to do that!

Expressions

be used to   *to be accustomed to*
Pete is **used to** being in high places because he's a
fireman.
Martha is not **used to** having problems with her
schoolwork.

give (someone) a hand   *to help (someone)*
Mrs. Vega asks Pete to **give her a hand** in getting her
kitten Snowy.
Do you have time to **give me a hand** with this heavy
box?

just a minute   *please wait (when used alone)*

Pete responds, "**Just a minute**," because he needs to get his ladder first.

I have to get my wallet before we leave. **Just a minute**.

lend (someone) a hand   *to help (someone), to give assistance*

Pete is glad to **lend a hand** in getting Snowy out of the tree.

No one was available to **lend** Max **a hand** in moving his possessions.

pitch in   *to help, to assist*

The interviewer is glad to **pitch in** and hold the ladder for Pete.

Good neighbors always **pitch in** when a serious situation arises.

Interview

The interviewer is helping as Pete climbs up the tree to rescue Snowy.

Mrs. Vega: **Take it easy**, Pete. It's dangerous up there. **Look out for** all of those small branches!

Pete: Yes, ma'am. I can handle it. Ouch!

Mrs. Vega: Poor Snowy. I can hear her **crying out** for help.

Pete: Don't worry, I can . . . Ouch! Don't scratch, Snowy. **Take it easy**, Snowy.

Mrs. Vega: I'm so glad you were **on hand**, Pete.

Pete: Well, here you are, Mrs. Vega. Here's Snowy, **safe and sound**.

Mrs. Vega: Thanks, Pete. But those scratches look pretty bad.

Pete: Not really, but I have to warn you— I'll never **take part in** this kind of animal rescue again.

Mrs. Vega: Oh? Why?

Int: I know why. Pete hates cats!

Expressions

cry out for   *to speak very loudly, to yell or shout*
Mrs. Vega can hear her kitten Snowy **crying out for** help.
The small child **cried out for** his mother when he got lost in the store.

look out for   *to be alert for, to be careful of*
Mrs. Vega warns Pete to **look out for** the small branches in the tree.
It's important to **look out for** cars when you cross the street.

on hand   *available, accessible*
Mrs. Vega is glad that Pete was **on hand** to help her out.
Many students keep their dictionary **on hand** at all times.

safe and sound   *completely safe or secure*
Pete is able to get Snowy down **safe and sound**.
The small child felt **safe and sound** in her bed
during the terrible storm.

take it easy   *to be careful; to stay calm*
Mrs. Vega warns Pete to **take it easy** while climbing
in the tree.
There's no reason to get upset about the accident.
Take it easy.

take part in   *to participate in,*
          to be involved in
Pete says that he will never again **take part in** the
rescue of a cat.
Hundreds of people were interested in **taking part in**
the Hollywood movie.

EXERCISE 1

Select the correct idiom to complete each sentence.

1. Everyone in the family _____ to decorate the
   Christmas tree.
   a. pitched in
   b. lent hands
   c. cried out for

2. I always keep a few extra dollars _____ for an
   emergency.
   a. safe and sound
   b. on hand
   c. giving me a hand

3. About twelve students will _____ the school play
   this weekend.
   a. lend a hand
   b. be used to
   c. take part in

4. You're driving too fast on this wet road. You
   should _____!
   a. safe and sound
   b. take it easy
   c. just a minute

5. Fred doesn't want to live with a roommate. He
   _____ living alone.
   a. cries out for
   b. gives himself a hand
   c. is used to

EXERCISE 2

**Fill in the blanks with the correct idiom. Each idiom is
used only once.**

on hand	pitch in	safe and sound
just a minute	giving me a hand	am used to

A: Todd, I certainly appreciate your _____
carrying those boxes.

B: Of course, Lisa. I'm always glad to _____.

A: You didn't have any difficulty carrying those big
boxes, did you?

B: No, I _____ lifting heavy things. I do
weightlifting twice a week.

A: Is that right? Well, anyway, I'm glad the boxes are
_____ here in my locked apartment.

B: Say, I'm thirsty. Do you have any soda drinks
_____?

A: I certainly do. _____ and I'll get some
from the refrigerator.

Lesson **2**

Decisions

Interview

The interview is talking to George Taylor and Alice Young, senior managers at Bond Textile Company.

Int: Thank you both for allowing me to **sit in on** this meeting. George, what problems are you **working out** these days?

George: Oh, we've got **a number** of problems. Alice can probably explain them to you better than I can.

Alice: Basically, we are trying to **think up** ways to **cut down on** production costs. They're really too high.

Int: Do you have any idea how you're going to do that?

Alice: We're going to have to **make the best use of** our new cutting machines.

George: Unfortunately, that means that some employees will lose their jobs.

65

Expressions

a number of   *several*
The Bond Textile Company has **a number of** problems to solve.
A number of people were unable to show up at the meeting.

cut down on   *to reduce, to lower*
Alice and George have to figure out a way to **cut down on** production costs.
The sick man had to **cut down on** smoking because he had trouble breathing.

make the best use of   *to use to maximum ability,*
                         to take advantage to the
                         greatest degree
By taking notes in class you **make the best use of** your time.
Make the best use of your savings and invest them in real estate.

sit in on   *to join as an observer*
The interviewer has been invited to **sit in on** the managers' meeting.
The high school principal **sat in on** the teachers' meeting about salaries.

think up   *to invent, to create,*
                    to discover
George and Alice have to **think up** ways to reduce production costs.
The young boy tried to **think up** an excuse for being late to school, but he couldn't **think** one **up**.

work out   *to solve, to plan*
Alice and George are trying to **work out** a number of problems these days.

We were able to **work out** all the details for our vacation.

Interview

The interviewer continues his conversation with George and Alice.

Int: Are there any problems you've already managed to **iron out**?

Alice: Yes, we've been able to **bring about** some important changes in our safety procedures.

George: Yes, I know something about that. Last month we **put forth** new safety standards for operating all of our equipment, but especially the cutting machines.

Int: Did you meet with the employees to come up with them?

Alice: We sure did, and those were some meetings! At times they went **on and on**, but eventually we **ended up** with a very good set of safety standards.

George: Yes, we don't think that our competitors can **come close to** our safety record since the standards were instituted last year.

Expressions

bring about   *to cause, to make happen*
The Bond Textile Company has **brought about** some important changes in safety procedures.
Do you know who **brought** the accident **about**?

come close to   *to approximate, to match*
The company's competitors can't **come close to** the new safety record.
The student's answer didn't **come close to** the right one.

end up   *to conclude, to finish*
After many meetings, the company **ended up** with excellent safety standards.
The meeting started in a classroom and **ended up** in the cafeteria.

iron out   *to solve, to work out*
Alice and George have managed to **iron out** some company problems.
The unhappy couple met with a counselor to **iron out** their marital difficulties.

on and on   *continuously,*
                            without stopping
Some of the company meetings with employees seemed to go **on and on**.
Mary likes to talk **on and on** when we chat on the telephone.

put forth   *to present, to propose*
Last month the company **put forth** new safety standards for equipment operation.

The president **put forth** an unusual plan for increasing product sales.

EXERCISE 1

Select the correct idiom to complete each sentence.

1. The engineers _____ a serious problem in the project proposal.
   a. worked out
   b. sat in on
   c. came close to

2. If Jeff hurries to write his paper, he'll _____ a poor grade on it.
   a. iron out
   b. think up
   c. end up with

3. The boring lecturer went _____ about his many accomplishments.
   a. cutting down
   b. on and on
   c. a number

4. The child _____ a good excuse for coming home late.
   a. thought up
   b. brought about
   c. sat in on

5. The company managers _____ new guidelines for employee sick leave.
   a. cut down on
   b. came close to
   c. put forth

EXERCISE 2

Fill in the blanks with the correct idiom. Each idiom is used only once.

on and on	a number of	sit in on
thought up	cut down on	put forth
work out	come close to	

The high school board of directors recently
_____ a new salary agreement for the
teachers to consider. Unfortunately, _____
the teachers thought that the proposal did not
_____ the changes that they expected. The
teachers had a meeting to _____ a response
to the administration proposal. They invited the
school principal to _____ their meeting
and offer advice. The meeting went _____
until late at night, but finally they _____ a
good plan. If the teachers could _____
their amount of sick leave, then there would be extra
money for the salary increase.

Problems and Solutions   MODULE 3

Lesson 3

Aches and Pains

Interview

The interviewer is talking to Jean Davis, a university
health clinic doctor, who is examining Jerry Moran,
a young student with an injured foot.

Int:	Do you mind, Doctor, if I **look on** while you're working?
Dr. Davis:	No, I don't mind. Jerry, please **pull up** your pants and **take off** your shoe and sock. I'll have to **wash off** your foot.
Int:	How did you hurt your foot, Jerry?
Jerry:	I was **playing catch** with a friend and I stepped on some broken glass.
Dr. Davis:	**I'm all through with** your bandage now, Jerry. I think you can **take care of** it by yourself, but see me again in three days.
Jerry:	Right, Dr. Davis. Thanks a lot.

71

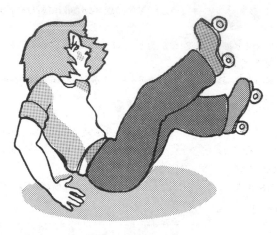

Expressions

be all through with *to be done with,*
to have finished with

Soon Dr. Davis **is all through with** putting on the bandage.

When you **are all through with** your homework, let's go outside to play.

look on *to observe, to watch*

The interviewer **looks on** as the doctor treats the student's injured foot.

Thousands of fans **looked on** as their team won the soccer tournament.

play catch *to throw a ball from one*
person to another

Jerry was **playing catch** with friends when he injured his foot.

Mike and his brother went in the back yard to **play catch** together.

pull up *to raise, to pull upwards*

Doctor Davis asks Jerry to **pull up** his pants so that his leg is showing.

Please **pull** your shirt sleeve **up** and the nurse will clean your wound.

take care of   *to be responsible for,*
to protect
Jerry can **take care of** his injury by himself for the next three days.
After school, Betty helps her mother **take care of** her baby sister.

take off   *to remove from the body*
Jerry has to **take off** his shoe and sock so that Dr. Davis can see his injured foot.
Please **take** your jacket **off** and sit down on the couch.

wash off   *to cleanse*
Dr. Davis has to **wash off** Jeff's foot because it's dirty.
After playing football, she had to **wash** the dirt **off** of her body.

Interview

The interviewer continues his conversation with Dr. Davis after the student leaves.

      Int: What are the usual problems you have to face?

Dr. Davis: Usually students are **under the weather** with the flu or some virus. In the winter, students **catch colds** a lot. There is always **something the matter**. We see them all here in the clinic.

      Int: What do you do if the student is really ill?

Dr. Davis: As I said, most of the students have minor problems. If a student **takes a turn for the worse**, however, we may

> have to put them in the university hospital.

Int: You seem to enjoy working with these young people.

Dr. Davis: I really do. We get to know **one another** well. Even after graduation, it's our policy to **follow up on** their health for as long as necessary.

Expressions

catch (a) cold(s)   *to become ill with a cold*
Many students **catch colds** in the wintertime.
If you stay outside in the rain, you'll probably **catch a cold**.

follow up on   *to continue one's involvement in*
The doctors at the health clinic **follow up on** the health of their patients.
The assistant was asked by her supervisor to **follow up on** the matter of the missing file.

one another   *between two or more people*
The doctors and student patients get to know **one another** quite well.
Gina and Mario love **one another** very much and are planning to get married next month.

something the matter   *something that is wrong*
There is always **something the matter** with the health of students at the university.
You don't look very happy. Is **something the matter**?

take a turn for the worse *to become more seriously ill*
When a student **takes a turn for the worse**, he or she may be sent to the university hospital.

All of our family relatives hurried to the nursing home when my ailing mother **took a turn for the worse**.

under the weather   *sick, in poor health*
Most students come to the clinic because they are **under the weather** with the flu or some virus.
You should go to bed early if you feel **under the weather**.

EXERCISE 1

Select the correct idiom to complete each sentence.

1. Mark was recovering from his illness, but then he
   _____.
   a. was all through with
   b. followed up on it
   c. took a turn for the worse

2. Mr. Barnes used soap to _____ the paint that had gotten on his arms.
   a. pull up
   b. look on
   c. wash off

3. Bob and Sarah know _____ very well. They've been dating for months.
   a. one other
   b. all through with
   c. something the matter

4. Would you ____ the baby while I shop at the store briefly?
   a. pull up
   b. look on
   c. take care of
5. Bea's supervisor was glad that Bea ____ the important assignment so well.
   a. followed up on
   b. took off
   c. was all through

EXERCISE 2

Fill in the blanks with the correct idiom. Each idiom is used only once.

under the weather   take care of
something the matter pull up
all through with   took a turn for the worse
coming down with   play catch

A: Mike, I'm _____ the household chores. Let's go outside and _____ together. I've got the ball and gloves.

B: I don't think so. I feel somewhat _____. I think I'm _____ with another cold.

A: Really? That's too bad. I thought you were getting better.

B: So did I. I tried my best to _____ myself by resting and taking medicine. But last night I _____ and felt worse.

A: There must be _____ with your health. Maybe you should see a doctor.

B: No, he'd just make me _____ my shirt and then he'd listen to my breathing. I hate that.

A: Why?
B: The instrument is too cold on my chest!

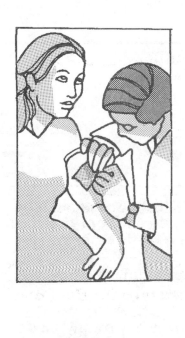

Lesson **4**

The Unexpected

Interview

The interviewer is talking again to Pete Martin, the fireman who got Mrs. Vega's cat down from the tree. Pete recently received a special award for bravery.

Int: Pete, would you mind telling me how you got the award for bravery?

Pete: It's a funny story. Every day on my way home I **go by** the Master Pet Store. I like to look in the window at the new puppies. I've been **toying with the idea of** buying a dog for the family.

Int: Is that when you saw the store **catch fire**?

Pete: No, I arrived shortly after it started. **In a moment**, however, it had turned into a large blaze.

Int: What did you do then?

Pete: Well it was hard to **get into** the store. The heat was bad. I had to **turn back** twice because of the smoke.

Expressions

catch fire	*to ignite, to start to burn*

Pete Martin was not near the store when it **caught fire**.

A tree can **catch fire** when lightning strikes it.

get into	*to enter; to be admitted to*

It was hard for Pete to **get into** the store because of the intense heat.

Pamela **got into** Harvard University on the basis of her academic achievements.

go by	*to pass, to move along*

Pete **goes by** the Master Pet Store every day on his way home.

Most children learn to appreciate what their parents say as time **goes by**.

in a moment	*soon, in a short period of time*

Pete was surprised that the fire became very serious **in a moment**.

I'll have an answer to this problem **in a moment**.

toy with the idea of   *to consider, to think about*
Pete has been **toying with the idea** of buying a dog for his family.
Jane **toyed with the idea** of not attending class, but then she decided to go.

turn back   *to return,*
to retrace one's steps
The heat and smoke in the building forced Pete to **turn back** twice.
The road was so dangerous that we had to **turn back**.

turn into   *to become*
The fire **turned into** a large blaze within a few minutes.
It's cloudy now, but it may **turn into** a nice day later.

Interview

The interviewer continues his conversation with Pete.

Int: Wasn't it dangerous inside?

Pete: Yes, it was, but the dogs were barking **like crazy** and I just couldn't ignore them. I **was in and out** of the store about ten times. The heat was bad, but I just had to **let** those animals **out**.

Int: Did you get them all out?

Pete: Yes, I did. But when I put the animals outside, they all **ran away**, of course. The fire department took more than two hours to bring all those loose animals back.

Int:　It **took guts** to do what you did.

Pete:　Not really. It took more courage to get Mrs. Vega's cat out of the tree!

Expressions

be in and out　　　　　*to enter and exit repeatedly*
Pete **was in and out** of the store several times to save the dogs.
Mr. Mason will **be in and out** of the office all day. Would you like to leave a message?

let out　　　　　*to release, to free*
Pete was able to **let out** all the animals without harm.
The cat is asking to go outside. Could you **let** it **out**?

like crazy　　　　　*madly, wildly, intensely*
We ran **like crazy** to catch the plane.
He'll have to **study like crazy** to pass the exam.

run away　　　　　*to flee, to escape*
All the dogs **ran away** as soon as Pete let them go outside.
The frightened girl tried to **run away** from the thief who wanted her purse.

take guts　　　　　*to require bravery or courage*
It **took guts** for Pete to save the animals under such dangerous conditions.
I think it **took a lot of guts** for Mark to admit that he was responsible for the mistake.

EXERCISE 1

Select the correct idiom to complete each sentence.

1. After Aaron became manager, he _____ a difficult person to work with.
   a. turned into
   b. toyed with the idea of
   c. brought back

2. If you wait for me, I'll be back _____.
   a. in and out
   b. in a moment
   c. running away

3. It _____ for Matthew to ride in a rollercoaster after years of being afraid.
   a. got into
   b. let out
   c. took guts

4. It's not possible to _____ the past, no matter how hard you try.
   a. bring back
   b. catch fire
   c. go by

5. It is not easy to _____ Harvard or MIT.
   a. go by
   b. get into
   c. be in and out

EXERCISE 2

Fill in the blanks with the correct idiom. Each idiom is used only once.

bringing back	took guts	in a moment
running away	caught fire	going by
turn back	turned into	like crazy
toyed with the idea of		

One day I was _____ some stores when I
smelled smoke. I decided to _____ and
check if a building had _____. I looked
down a side street and saw a man running _____
I thought that he might be a criminal that was
_____ and I _____ calling the police
right away. However, _____ I changed my
mind and decided to go to the back of the building
and investigate. The man was _____ a
water hose to extinguish the fire in his store. He
asked for my help in controlling the fire before it
_____ a serious one. It _____
for us to fight the fire and heat inside, but
fortunately we succeeded before a disaster occurred.

Module 3 Review

EXERCISE 1

Select the correct idiom for the boldface phrase or word.

1. **Please wait** while I get my hat and coat from the closet.
   a. In a minute
   b. Just a minute
   c. on and on

2. The new manager **caused** an improvement in work conditions.
   a. pitched in
   b. brought about
   c. wound up with

3. Steve **considered** postponing his vacation for two weeks, but then decided against it.
   a. toyed with the idea of
   b. took it easy
   c. came close to

4. Ellen agreed to **continue to monitor** the project she had started.
   a. follow up on
   b. iron out
   c. look out for

5. The baby felt **completely secure** in its mother's arms.
   a. on hand
   b. something the matter
   c. safe and sound

6. Would you please **stay calm** so that we can solve this problem?
   a. take guts
   b. lend a hand
   c. take it easy

7. **Several** persons complained about the loud noise coming from the party.
   a. one another
   b. a number of
   c. on hand

8. I used the washing machine when my roommate **was finished with** it.
   a. was used to
   b. cut down on
   c. was all through with

9. The dog is asking to be **released**; please open the door for it.
   a. let out
   b. put forth
   c. taken off

10. After all of our effort, we **concluded** with a very successful fund-raising event.
   a. cried out for
   b. ended up
   c. turned into

EXERCISE 2

Write a short story for each picture by using the suggested idioms. You may use other idioms as well.

1. (pictures, page 64)
   let out, cry out for, something the matter,
   run away

---

2. (pictures, page 64)
    pitch in, take guts, take it easy, safe and sound

---

3. (top picture, page 77)
    pull up, wash off, take care of, in a moment

---

4. (middle picture, page 77)
    play catch, one another, look on, come close to

Human Relationships **MODULE 4**

Lesson **1**

Friendship

The interviewer is talking to Leigh and Kate, two ten-year-old girls who go to the same school.

Int: Kate, I want to ask how you and Leigh met. How did you **make friends** with one another?

Kate: Well, last year at school some boys tried to **take away** my bike.

Leigh: And I **ran after** them and made them **give it back**. Kate was so happy that she shared her lunch with me. We've been friends ever since.

Kate: Yes, that's what happened. That's why Leigh is my friend. I can **count on** her **through thick and thin**.

Int: And I'm sure that you can **count on** Kate, too.

Expressions

count on　　　　　　*to rely on, to trust*
Kate and Leigh are fortunate that they can **count on** one another.
You can **count on** Jan to be prepared to teach class well.

give back　　　　　　*to return something*
Leigh made the boys at school **give back** Kate's bicycle.
I'll **give** your book **back** tomorrow, if that's okay with you.

make friends　　　　　*to become friends*
Kate and Leigh **made friends** with one another at school.
Our new neighbors are nice people; it's been easy to **make friends** with them.

run after　　　　　　*to chase, to pursue*
Leigh **ran after** the boys who tried to take Kate's bike.

The police **ran after** the thief who was seen taking a TV out of a house.

take away   *to remove, to take from*
Some boys **took away** Kate's bike on the way to school.
Sometimes it seems that the government **takes** all our money **away** in taxes.

through thick and thin   *through good and bad times*
Kate and Leigh can count on each other **through thick and thin**.
Through thick and thin, our family will always stay close together.

Interview

The interviewer continues his conversation with Leigh and Kate.

Int: What kinds of things do you both like to do?

Leigh: We like to **go for walks** a lot and talk about our friends. Sometimes Kate comes home with me after school and we ride our skateboards. We just like to **hang out** together.

Kate: And we like to **make up** stories about what we'll be doing when we grow up—like having parties and **going out** to restaurants and to the movies.

Int: Do you think that you'll still be friends when you **grow up**?

Kate: Oh, yes. That's still **a long way off**, but I know we'll always be friends.

Expressions

a (little or long) way off *within a relatively short or long time*
It's still **a long way off** before Leigh and Kate become adults.
It's spring now, and summer is only **a little way off**.

go for (a) walk(s) *to stroll leisurely*
Kate and Leigh enjoy **going for walks** together and talking.
What a lovely day! Would you like to **go for a walk**?

go out *to leave home or work*
Kate and Leigh aren't old enough to **go out** alone to restaurants or the movies.
Mr. Lee **went out** for lunch and will be back in an hour. Would you like to wait?

grow up *to become mature*
When Kate and Leigh **grow up**, they'll have their own parties and go out a lot.
Sometimes children are too eager to **grow up**; they should enjoy their childhood while it lasts.

hang out *to associate, to do things*
Kate and Leigh spend a lot of time just **hanging out** together.
During the summer my friends and I stayed in San Diego and **hung out** at the beach.

make up *to invent, to fabricate*
Kate and Leigh like to **make up** stories about what they'll do when they grow up.
Jim tried to **make up** a good excuse for being late, but he couldn't think one up.

EXERCISE 1

Select the correct idiom to complete each sentence.

1. When I _____, I'd like to become a doctor.
   a. make up
   b. make friends
   c. grow up

2. It's such a nice day. Let's _____ in the park.
   a. run away
   b. take away
   c. go for a walk

3. The police had to _____ the thief who ran away
   down a side street.
   a. count on
   b. run after
   c. go out

4. When are you going to _____ the ten dollars that
   you borrowed from me?
   a. give back
   b. make up
   c. take away

5. Whenever Jim needs help, he can _____ his
   parents.
   a. make friends with
   b. through thick or thin
   c. count on

EXERCISE 2

Fill in the blanks with the correct idiom. Each idiom is used only once.

given...back	a little way off	go for a walk
take away	grow up	count on
made friends with	through thick and thin	

A: Would you like to _____ along the beach this morning?

B: Isn't the furniture company coming to _____ your broken couch?

A: They're coming at eleven, so that's _____. We have time.

B: Good. By the way, have you _____ with the new neighbor?

A: No, not yet. I met him briefly a week ago when he borrowed a pot and pan. He hasn't _____ them _____ yet.

B: It's strange how you can't _____ some people. They act without responsibility, like children, and never seem to _____.

A: It's good to know that the two of us will stay together _____!

Lesson **2**

Love and Affection

Interview

The interviewer is talking to Everett and Marion
Hale, who have been married for forty years.

Int: Marion, when did you first meet
Everett?

Marion: In high school. I knew him for a long
time before we **fell in love**.

Int: Did you date him in high school?

Marion: No, I didn't. He was so strange **in those
days**. I think he was scared of my
parents.

Everett: I was always nervous **in front of** Marion's
parents. Her parents almost **drove** me
away.

Int: Why was that?

Marion: They were very careful about the boys I
dated. Many times I thought that it **was
all over** between us.

93

Expressions

be all over   *to be completely finished*
Sometimes Marion thought that her relationship
with Everett **was all over**.
I thought that it **was all over** for me when that large
truck almost hit me.

drive away   *to repel, to cause to leave*
Marion's parents almost **drove** Everett **away** because
of their careful attitude.
We keep dogs in our yard to **drive away** any
trespassers.

fall in love   *to begin to love*
Marion and Everett didn't **fall in love** until after
high school.
Some people meet, **fall in love**, and get married
within a short time.

in front of   *in the presence of, facing*
Everett always felt nervous while he was **in front of**
Marion's parents.

Don't use those bad words **in front of** the small
children!

in those days   *in the past, in past years*
In those days Everett acted strangely towards
Marion.
People used to read more **in those days** before television.

Interview

The interviewer continues his conversation with
Everett and Marion Hale.

Int: Did you only date one another?

Marion: Yes, I didn't have any other boyfriends.
Even when we had arguments, we always
made up.

Everett: We really **believed in** the old expression,
"It's better to kiss and **make up**."

Int: When did you know that you'd get
married?

Marion: Well, **by and by** I realized that I couldn't **keep from** loving him.

Everett: And I realized that she was the one for me.

Int: If you had to **go back** and do it over again, would you?

Marion/ Everett: Of course!

Expressions

believe in   *to trust, to have faith in*
Everett and Marion really **believe in** each other.
Do you **believe in** the principles of democracy?

by and by   *eventually, after a period of time*
By and by Marion realized that she loved Everett very much.
At first I hated her, but **by and by** I began to see that she had many good qualities.

go back   *to return to a place or time*
If Marion and Everett could **go back** and fall in love again, they would.
As you grow older, you sometimes want to **go back** to your childhood days.

keep from   *to avoid, to stop doing*
Marion and Everett couldn't **keep from** loving each other after a while.
To **keep from** smoking, I eat sugar-free candy all day.

make up   *to become friendly again (after a fight)*
After Marion and Everett had arguments, they always **made up**.

It's better to kiss and **make up** than to remain angry for long.

EXERCISE 1

Select the correct idiom to complete each sentence.

1. Mark was upset when he realized that his relationship with Ann _____.
   a. fell in love
   b. was all over
   c. made up

2. I grew up in the 1970's. _____, there weren't as many TV shows as now.
   a. by and by
   b. in front of
   c. in those days

3. Dick _____ with his brother after they argued about a large money expense.
   a. made up
   b. believed in
   c. drove away

4. Why don't you _____ to the store and complain about the mistake in pricing?
   a. go back
   b. keep from
   c. drive away

5. Vera _____ Todd after only a short period of time.
   a. was in front of
   b. fell in love with
   c. kept from

EXERCISE 2

Fill in the blanks with the correct idiom. Each idiom is used only once.

make up	in those days	go back
drive away	keep from	believe in
fall in love	are all over	by and by

In the 1950's, life was much simpler. _____, you could _____ your neighbors without doubt. If you had a girlfriend, you would _____ and get married only after a long period of dating. You'd probably_____ kissing her in public. _____ things have changed. Now you might _____ your girlfriend or wife after only one argument, and then refuse to _____. Some people would like to _____ to the good days, but it is obvious that those days _____.

Lesson **3**

Strangers

Interview

The interviewer is talking to James Willis, a businessman who has recently come to the interviewer's city to work for one year.

Int: James, I'd like to ask you some questions about what you think of our city.

James: Sure. What's **on your mind**?

Int: I know you're **new in town** and I would like to know if you've had any problems getting used to life here.

James: No, not really. The people here **go out of their way** to be friendly. They don't want to **leave** anyone **out in the cold**.

Int: I'm glad to hear it. Since you **come from** New York City, I thought you might **feel funny** in a small town.

EXPRESSIONS

be new in town   *to be a stranger*
James recently arrives from New York City and **is new in town**.
I'm new in town. Could you recommend a good hotel?

be on one's mind   *to occupy one's*
                     thoughts or attention
Because James doesn't know what questions the interviewer will ask, he asks the interviewer, "What**'s on your mind**?"
She**'s on my mind** all the time because I've fallen deeply in love with her.

come from   *to originate from,*
                     to be born and raised in
James **comes from** New York City, where people are not very friendly.
I **come from** a small town, but my wife comes from a major U.S. city.

100

feel funny   *to feel uncomfortable*
                          or awkward

After living in New York City, it's possible that James
feels funny in a small town.

She's a strange person. Everyone **feels funny** when
she's present.

go out of one's way   *to make a special effort*

People in a small town **go out of their way** to be
friendly to visitors.

Martha **went out of her way** to make our stay in her
home comfortable.

leave out in the cold   *to ignore, not to*
                               pay attention to

Small town people don't want to **leave** any visitor **out
in the cold.**

Ann was **left out in the cold** when her friends had a
party without her.

Interview

The interviewer continues his conversation with
James Willis.

> **Int:**   I bet that you are glad not to **feel left out**
> in our community.

> **James:** Well, actually, in New York I was used to
> living **by myself**, so I don't need a lot of
> company.

> **Int:**   But here people love to have guests.

> **James:** I know. **As a matter of fact**, people here
> never **leave** me **alone**! I'm not used to so
> much attention.

> **Int:**   We just want you to **feel at home**.

James: I know, and I'm not complaining. It's just that I've **shaken hands** so many times, my hand is sore. I can barely hold a fork while I eat!

Expressions

as a matter of fact   *actually, really*
As a matter of fact, James is probably receiving more attention than he wants.
Why do you think that I dislike him? **As a matter of fact**, I think he's really nice.

by oneself   *alone, without help*
Because James comes from a big city, he's used to living **by himself**.
The Thompsons are skilled craftspeople. They built their home **by themselves**.

feel at home   *to feel comfortable,*
          to feel welcomed
The people in the small town want James to **feel at home**.
Everyone in this neighborhood is so friendly. I **feel** right **at home**.

feel left out   *to feel rejected or excluded*
It's hard for someone to **feel left out** in the interviewer's community.
When John wasn't invited to your birthday party, he **felt left out**.

leave alone   *not to bother,*
          to permit to be alone
James wishes that sometimes people would just **leave** him **alone**.
Would you please **leave** me **alone**? I'm busy right now.

shake hands　　　*to greet other people by*
　　　　　　　　　clasping right hands

James has **shaken hands** with almost everybody in town.

We **shook hands** when we first met and also when we left.

Exercise 1

Select the correct idiom to complete each sentence.

1. Jim _____ when he wasn't invited to the high school reunion.
   a. went out of his way
   b. felt at home
   c. felt left out

2. Terry has a strange accent. I wonder where she _____.
   a. is new in town
   b. comes from
   c. was left out in the cold

3. I _____ at the reception because I was the only one without a suit and tie.
   a. felt funny
   b. shook hands
   c. was on my mind

4. Would you please _____ while I finish this important work?
   a. leave me alone
   b. by myself
   c. go out of your way

5. Stephen looked very worried, so I asked him what _____.
   a. was a matter of fact
   b. made him feel at home
   c. was on his mind

EXERCISE 2

Fill in the blanks with the correct idiom. Each idiom is used only once.

new in town   by yourself   as a matter of fact
feel funny   come from   feel at home
is on your mind

A: Ted, don't you want to go to the party?

B: _____, I don't. You should go
_____.

A: Don't say that. I would _____ if I went alone.

B: That's just it. We're both _____. No one knows us at all.

A: I'm sure they would try to make us
_____.

B: How? By asking stupid questions about our backgrounds, like where we _____?

A: Come on, Ted, tell me what really _____.

B: Well, I'd rather stay home and watch my favorite movie on TV!

Lesson 4

Disappointment and Regret

Interview

The interviewer is talking to two high school students, Samuel and Millie, about the worst thing that ever happened to them.

Int: And what's the worst thing that ever happened to you?

Samuel: The worst thing was when I broke up with my girlfriend. It almost **broke my heart.** Luckily, we made up and **got back together.**

Int: And you? What's the worst thing that happened to you?

Millie: Nothing really bad has ever happened. I guess last month I failed my driver's test because I didn't study. Everyone **looked down on** me. It was really embarrassing.

Samuel: The worst thing of all is to **be around** phony people. They can't do anything except criticize. They **find fault with** everything you do.

Expressions

be around *to be in the presence of, to associate with*

Samuel doesn't like to **be around** people who have phony characters.

When I**'m around** Elaine, I always seem to get nervous.

break one's heart *to hurt one's feelings deeply*

When Samuel broke up with his girlfriend, it nearly **broke his heart**.

It **broke my heart** when I moved into an apartment and had to sell my dog.

find fault with *to criticize, to complain about*

Phony people are often quick to **find fault with** other people.

Don't **find fault with** your friends because they'll always find fault with you!

get back together *to rejoin after making up*

Samuel and his girlfriend made up and **got back**

together again.
I'm so glad that Ellen and Jim **got back together**
instead of getting a divorce.

look down on   *to consider inferior, to scorn*
Everyone **looked down on** Millie when she failed her
driver's test.
You shouldn't **look down on** poor people; it's not
their choice to live in poverty.

Interview

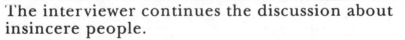

The interviewer continues the discussion about
insincere people.

    Int: How do you feel about phony people,
              Millie?

  Millie: I hate phonies too. A phony **puts up a
              front** and pretends to be your friend,
              and then tries to **take advantage of** you.

  Samuel: Phonies always try to **pull the wool over
              your eyes**. They also try to **show off** all
              the time because they think they're so
              important.

    Int: Are some of your friends like that?

> **Millie:** A few. I **feel sorry for** people like that. I
> think that early in life they must
> have **gotten off** on **the wrong foot.**

Expressions

feel sorry for   *to sympathize with*
Millie **feels sorry for** people who need attention and
who deceive others.
Sylvia has had such a hard life that everyone **feels
sorry for** her.

get off on the wrong foot   *to start poorly,*
                                   to make a blunder
Millie thinks that phony people must **get off on the
wrong foot** early in life.
When Charlie angered his new boss, he really **got off
on the wrong foot.**

put up a front   *to act insincerely*
A phony person **puts up a front** by pretending to be
someone he or she isn't.
Don't **put up a front** with me. I can tell that you're
not interested at all.

pull the wool over one's eyes   *to deceive, to lie*
Phony people often try to **pull the wool over your
eyes** for their own benefit.
Cindy **pulled the wool over my eyes** by lying about
her qualifications for the job.

show off   *to show one's special talents
                       in order to attract attention*
Phony people **show off** in front of others because
they think they're important.
If you don't pay attention to him, he won't **show off**
as much.

take advantage of   *to profit at the expense*
                             of another

Phony people try to **take advantage of** their friends on every occasion.

Our soccer team **took advantage of** the other team's mistakes and scored a goal.

EXERCISE 1

Select the correct idiom to complete each sentence.

1. Larry _____ at the school party by dancing on the auditorium stage.
   a. looked down on
   b. showed off
   c. put up a front

2. It _____ when I had to sell my car to pay some long-overdue bills.
   a. felt sorry for
   b. got back together
   c. broke my heart

3. Lynn tries to behave properly so that her parents don't _____ her.
   a. find fault with
   b. be around
   c. take advantage of

4. When we argued the first time we met, we _____.
   a. were around
   b. pulled the wool over our eyes
   c. got off on the wrong foot

5. Everyone _____ Walter because he's lied and cheated so many times.
   a. puts up a front
   b. is around
   c. looks down on

EXERCISE 2

Fill in the blanks with the correct idiom. Each idiom is used only once.

felt sorry for	look down on	showing off
took advantage of	was around	got off on the
putting up a front	finding fault with	wrong foot

When I first met Jose, we _____ by having an argument. It happened on the first day of school. Everyone _____ me because I was _____ my new karate skills. Then Jose, who was a new student, came up and started _____ my ability. He said that I didn't know karate at all and that I was _____. I got really angry and said that everyone would _____ him because he was fat. He got really upset too and we started fighting. I was bigger than Jose was, so I _____ my size and easily got him on the ground. Jose started crying and I let him go because I _____ him.

Module 4 Review

EXERCISE 1

Select the correct idiom for the boldface phrase.

1. If you **trust** your country, then you should obey its laws.
   a. believe in
   b. feel sorry for
   c. keep from

2. All summer Sue and her friends **did things** at the beach and just relaxed.
   a. drove away
   b. felt left out
   c. hung out

3. I really enjoyed the party. **Actually**, it was one of the best I've gone to this year.
   a. a little way off
   b. as a matter of fact
   c. by and by

4. Hank **acts insincerely** at school, but at home he's actually quite a different person.
   a. puts up a front
   b. grows up
   c. is around

5. Winter **is within a short period of time**, but already it's quite cold during the day.
   a. is all over
   b. is in those days
   c. is a little way off

6. When my children were very young, it was easy to
   decieve them.
   a. keep from them
   b. shake their hands
   c. pull the wool over their eyes

7. However, now my children are older and know
   when I'm trying to **profit at their expense**.
   a. make friends with them
   b. take advantage of them
   c. come from them

8. Ann's teacher **makes a special effort** to help her
   students whenever she can.
   a. goes out of her way
   b. feels left out
   c. goes back

9. You can **rely on me** to be your friend through thick
   and thin.
   a. leave me alone
   b. count on me
   c. run after me

10. If Mike **avoids** smoking and starts exercising, his
    health will improve.
    a. keeps from
    b. drives away
    c. breaks his heart

EXERCISE 2

**Write a short story for each picture by using the suggested
idioms. You may use other idioms as well.**

1. (left pictures, page 109)
   break one's heart, leave alone, go back, make up

_____
_____
_____
_____
_____
_____

2. (picture, page 107)
    be new in town, show off, drive away, feel left out)

_____
_____
_____
_____
_____
_____

3. (picture, page 110)
    pull the wool over one's eyes, find fault with, grow up,
    keep from

_____
_____
_____
_____
_____
_____

4. (right pictures, page 109)
    be around, take advantage of, by oneself, take away)

_____
_____
_____
_____
_____
_____

Lesson **1**

Making Plans

Interview

The interviewer is talking to Amy Taylor and Kathy Belli, who share an apartment and work in the same bank.

Int: Have you planned anything for the weekend?

Amy: Yes and no. I'd really like to **go on a trip**, but you can't travel **for nothing**, you know.

Int: What do you mean?

Kathy: She's trying to say that we**'re broke**. Besides, Amy, I don't feel like **going away**.

Amy: Well, okay. Maybe something interesting will **turn up** here in town.

Kathy: In that case, we'll just **play it by ear**.

Int: It sounds like you two get along very well!

114

Expressions

---

be broke   *to be without money*
Kathy and Amy **are broke** and cannot afford a vacation.
I'm sorry I can't loan you any money. **I'm broke** right now.

for nothing   *at no cost, for free*
It's impossible for Kathy and Amy to travel **for nothing**.
The grocer gave us some overripe bananas **for nothing**.

go away   *to leave town, to depart*
Kathy doesn't feel like **going away** for the weekend.
Ed and Mary **went away** for a quick vacation in the mountains.

go on a trip   *to travel*
Amy would really enjoy **going on a trip** if possible.
Jill is planning to **go on a trip** to Japan next summer.

play (it) by ear   *to do something without a clear plan, to improvise*

Amy and Kathy will wait to see what develops. They'll **play it by ear**.
Let's **play** our trip **by ear** this time instead of planning every aspect beforehand.

turn up   *to materialize, to be found*

Amy hopes that some interesting activity in town will **turn up**.
Don't worry about your car keys. I'm sure they'll **turn up** soon.

Interview

The interviewer continues the conversation with Amy and Kathy.

Int: Have you heard of the new movie in town called Earrings and Shoes?

Amy: Yes, I have. It's supposed to be **out of the ordinary**. In fact, the theater was so crowded last night that some people had to **stand up** in the back.

Kathy: I've been **looking forward** to seeing that movie. Maybe your sister can come with us.

Amy: I don't know. It's hard for her to get a babysitter **on short notice**.

Int: Well, I won't **take up** any more of your time. I know how hard it can be to find a babysitter.

Kathy: **Once in a while** she's lucky and finds a sitter right away!

Expressions

look forward to   *to anticipate with pleasure*
Kathy is **looking forward to** seeing the movie,
Earrings and Shoes.
My wife and I are **looking forward to** the party this
evening.

once in a while   *occasionally, sometimes*
Amy's sister is able to get a babysitter without
difficulty **once in a while**
Once in a while I get hungry between meals, so I
have candy bars on hand.

on (such) short notice   *within a limited time*
Sometimes it's hard to get a babysitter **on short
notice**.
I'm glad you could make it to the meeting **on such
short notice**.

out of the ordinary   *unusual*
The movie Earrings and Shoes is supposed to be **out
of the ordinary**.
Isn't it **out of the ordinary** for Sam to be late like
this?

stand up   *to remain standing, to rise*
The theater was so crowded that many people had to
stand up in the back.
Would you mind **standing up** for a moment so that I
can fix the couch cover?

take up   *to occupy*
                         (time, space, or resources)
The interviewer will leave and not **take up** any more
of their time.
Jim's model airplane hobby **takes up** most of the
space in our garage.

117

EXERCISE 1

Select the correct idiom to complete each sentence.

1. I need my wallet to go shopping. I hope it _____ soon.
   a. goes away
   b. turns up
   c. is broke

2. Jake had to leave town _____ to do business for his company.
   a. on short notice
   b. out of the ordinary
   c. for nothing

3. We've been sitting in class too long. I wish we could _____ briefly.
   a. play it by ear
   b. go on a trip
   c. stand up

4. How is Lenny going to pay his bills this month? He _____!
   a. is broke
   b. takes up
   c. turns up

5. The plumber honored the warranty and fixed the broken water heater _____.
   a. once in a while
   b. for nothing
   c. out or the ordinary

EXERCISE 2

Fill in the blanks with the correct idiom. Each idiom is used only once.

on short notice	looking forward to	turn up
out of the ordinary	was broke	for free
once in awhile	go on a trip	take up

I was really _____ to my last vacation.
However, I _____ again and couldn't afford to
_____ anywhere. As a result, I stayed home,
hoping for something interesting to _____. I
went to the park _____ for some exercise, or
sometimes to the beach to lie in the sun. Those
activities I could do _____. One day a
friend called _____ and suggested that we
go to a party in an hour. He said that it wouldn't
_____ too much of my time. I laughed
because I had nothing but time on my hands; it was
_____ for me to be busy.

Lesson **2**

Eating Out

Interview

The interviewer (Hugh) and a friend, Grace Leclerq, are at a local restaurant owned by Chuck Jordan, the interviewer's friend. The waiter is a new employee.

Waiter: Please sit down. As you requested, you have a view of the garden.

Int: Thank you. Grace, I'm sure you're going to like this place. I **eat out** quite a lot and I've never found fault with the food or service.

Waiter: Would you like to order now?

Int: We'd like to look over the menu a bit more . . . The roast beef **sounds good**.

Grace: I **would rather** have the broiled fish. I've been **putting on weight** recently. The fish would be better for my diet.

Int: Grace, you're so slim. You don't need to **be on a diet**.

Waiter: **Take your time** deciding, folks. I'll be back in a moment.

Expressions

be on a diet   *to diet, to try to lose weight*
Grace **is on a diet** to lose some weight.
I don't think I'll eat dessert because I'**m on a diet**.

eat out   *to eat away from home*
The interviewer likes to **eat out** often at local
restaurants.
With a large family and high food costs, we don't **eat
out** very often.

put on weight   *to gain weight,*
                          to increase in weight
Grace thinks that she has been **putting on weight**
recently.
Since Rose has stopped smoking, she has **put on
weight**.

sound good   *to be appealing, desirable*
The roast beef dinner **sounds good** to the
interviewer.
Are you offering to pay for the meal? That **sounds
good**!

121

take one's time   *not to be in a hurry*
Grace and Hugh should **take their time** deciding
what to eat.
Don't drive so fast. **Take your time** and enjoy the
view.

would rather   *to prefer to*
Grace **would rather** have fish than red meat for her
diet.
Would you **rather** eat at home or go out?

Interview

After the meal, the conversation with the waiter
continues.

Waiter: Was everything all right, sir?

Int: I'd like to see the manager.

Waiter: Er . . . yes, sir. I'll get him. I hope
everything was satisfactory.

Grace: What **are** you **up to**, Hugh?

Int: I'm just **playing a joke on** my friend
Chuck, who's the manager here.

Manager: I hope there's **nothing the matter**,
sir . . . Oh, it's you, Hugh!

Int: Hi, Chuck! As usual, everything was
wonderful. We especially enjoyed the
view **looking out on** the garden.

Manager: That's good, Hugh. And how was the
service of our new waiter, Larry?

Int: Larry's service was **nothing short of** excellent. We truly enjoyed ourselves.

Grace: That's right, Larry. And Hugh, since you're **picking up the tab**, I think that Larry deserves a big tip!

Expressions

---

be up to (something)   *to be planning, plotting, or scheming*

Grace wonders what Hugh **is up to** when he asks to talk to the manager.

I don't know what that child is doing. He must **be up to** something.

look out on   *to overlook, to have a view of*

Hugh and Grace are sitting at a table **looking out on** the garden.

Our house **looks out on** the ocean from the top of a hill.

nothing short of   *completely, thoroughly*

Hugh indicates that the waiter's service was **nothing short of** excellent.

This food is **nothing short of** superb. I've never tasted better.

nothing the matter   *nothing that is wrong*

The waiter hopes that there's **nothing the matter** with the service or food.

There's **nothing the matter** with the television. What happened?

pick up the tab   *to pay the bill, pay the cost of*

Grace expects Hugh to **pick up the tab** for the meal at the restaurant.

123

My company **picked up the tab** for all of my expenses at the conference.

play (a) joke(s) on   *to trick, to tease*
Hugh is trying to **play a joke** on his friend the manager and the waiter.
My brother loves to **play jokes on** me. He teases me all the time.

EXERCISE 1

Select the correct idiom to complete each sentence.

1. The weather we had on vacation was _____ fantastic.
   a. nothing the matter
   b. sounding good
   c. nothing short of

2. Don't eat so fast! _____ and enjoy the meal.
   a. Be on a diet
   b. Take your time
   c. Look out on

3. My wife and I like to _____ so that we don't have to cook and wash dishes.
   a. be on a diet
   b. pick up the tab
   c. eat out

4. Connie _____ me by pretending that I had won some money in the lottery.
   a. played a joke on
   b. picked up the tab for
   c. sounded good for

5. He hasn't told anyone about his plan. I wonder what he _____.
   a. is up to
   b. is nothing the matter
   c. would rather

EXERCISE 2

Fill in the blanks with the correct idiom. Each idiom is used only once.

would rather	on a diet	take your time
put on weight	nothing short of	sound good
nothing the matter		

A: Boy, I'm eating too much. I'm glad I'm not
 _____ anymore.

B: Oh, did you _____ before? Your physical
 condition looks _____ excellent.

A: Well, thank you. It's true that there's _____
 with my body. I'm just starting to get full.

B: If you _____ eating, you won't get so full.
 Are you almost ready for dessert?

A: Oh, I _____ not have any. But some coffee
 would _____.

Lesson **3**

Entertainment

Interview

The interviewer is talking to some people on the street about their entertainment choices.

Int: What do you do to have a good time, sir?

Husband: Oh, we go out dancing and eating. My wife and I **step out** at least twice a week. We really **live it up**, don't we, Nancy?

Wife: Yes, we do. We usually **stay out** until two or three in the morning. We really **have a ball**.

Int: Aren't you tired by that time?

Wife: Yes, often I am, but I have to **keep my eye on** my husband. He tries to **pig out** at the restaurant and dance with other women!

Husband: Nancy, that's not true. I'm not overweight and I don't flirt.

Wife: Thanks to me!

Expressions

have a ball   *to have a lot of fun*
The couple **have a ball** when they go out for the
evening.
The children **had a ball** at the circus yesterday.

keep one's eye on   *to observe or watch*
                               constantly
The woman must **keep her eye on** her husband's
eating and social habits.
Please **keep your eye on** the children at the
playground.

live it up   *to enjoy life fully,*
                               to spend extravagantly
The couple **live it up** as often as they can afford to.
On our vacation, we stayed at a five-star hotel and
really **lived it up**.

pig out   *to eat too much food*
The man has a tendency to **pig out** when he has a
chance.

If you **pig out** on the cake, there won't be enough for everybody.

stay out   *to remain away from home*
The couple often **stays out** until two or three in the morning.
Mother told me that I could **stay out** until midnight with my friends.

step out   *to seek entertainment*
                             outside the home
The couple **steps out** at least twice a week by going out to eat and dance.
We aren't able to **step out** as often as before because we have children.

Interview

The interviewer continues his conversation with other people. It's raining.

Int: And you, sir, what do you do for fun?

Man: Oh, I love baseball. In fact, I'm **on my way to** the game right now.

Int: Baseball is my favorite too. You know, if this rain doesn't **let up** soon, the game may be **called off**.

Man: Yes, I know. I'm going to **take a chance**, though. I've had these tickets for a week. Nice talking to you.

Int: Excuse me, ma'am. I'm asking people what they do for entertainment.

Woman: Oh, I like to **take in** a movie at least once a week.

Int: Is there any movie you really want to see now?

Woman: Yes, I **have my heart set on** seeing Lost Paradise.

Int: I heard it's good. Well, thanks very much!

Expressions

be on one's way to   *be going to*
The man **is on his way** to a baseball game when the interviewer stops him.
If you**'re on your way** to the supermarket, could you buy some milk?

call off   *to cancel*
The baseball game may be **called off** because of the weather.
The president had to leave town, so he **called** the meeting **off**.

have one's heart set on   *to want or desire something very much*
The woman **has her heart set on** seeing a new movie.
Susan **had her heart set on** a trip to Europe, but she couldn't afford it.

let up   *to decrease, to slacken*
If the rain **lets up**, the baseball game won't be cancelled.
If the wind doesn't **let up** soon, we should postpone our picnic.

take (a) chance(s)   *to risk, to gamble*
The man is **taking a chance** on going to the game because he already has tickets.

The young people **took chances** when they climbed up the steep, rocky hill.

take in   *to attend, to experience*
The woman likes to **take in** a movie at least once a week.
The tour group participants **took in** all the sights of Rome in just three days.

EXERCISE 1

Select the correct idiom to complete each sentence.

1. You'll get sick if you ____ late every night.
   a. stay out
   b. call off
   c. let up

2. I stopped by the bank _____ work this morning.
   a. taking a chance on
   b. on my way to
   c. calling off

3. Martha didn't want to _____ last night because she _____ watching a movie on TV.
   a. pig out
   b. have a ball
   c. step out

4. She _____ winning the first prize.
   a. kept her eye on
   b. had her heart set on
   c. took a chance on

5. I hope the storm _____ so that we can go outside and play.
   a. lets up
   b. lives it up
   c. takes in

130

EXERCISE 2

Fill in the blanks with the correct idiom. Each idiom is used only once.

live it up	let up	take a chance
had a ball	call off	step out
stayed out	kept our eye on	pigged out

Last night my girlfriend and I wanted to _____
for something to eat, but the rain wouldn't
_____. We didn't want to _____ of
getting wet, so we waited for a while. We _____
the condition of the weather outside, hoping for a
change. While we waited, we _____ on
potato chips and beer. We were about to _____
our plans when the rain suddenly stopped, so we left
right away. We decided to go to an expensive
restaurant and really to _____. Afterwards we
went to a nightclub to dance; we _____ until
after midnight and _____!

Lesson **4**

Preparing for Bed

Interview

The interviewer is talking to Gina Novak, who is tired after a long day of teaching at a ballet school.

Int: I'll bet you're glad that this day has **come to an end**.

Gina: You're right. I taught ballet classes all day long. **At last** I can relax.

Int: Will you **stay up** for a while or sleep right away?

Gina: Oh, I'll stay up and do some things first.

Int: Do you have a nightly routine?

Gina: Oh, yes. First I have to **put out** the fire in the fireplace and **put away** my dancing things. Then I **let in** the cat.

Int: I bet the cat would never forgive you for leaving it outside!

Expressions

at last   *finally*
Gina can relax **at last** after a hard day at work.
At last I'm all done with this difficult assignment.

come to an end   *to be completely finished*
Gina is glad that this day has **come to an end**.
We liked the movie so much that we were sorry when
it **came to an end**.

let in   *to allow to enter*
Gina makes sure to **let in** her cat before going to
bed.
When the dog barks at the door, could you **let** it **in**?

put away   *to store in the proper place*
Gina has a lot of dancing items to **put away** when she
gets home.
I told the children to **put** their toys **away** before
coming down for dinner.

134

put out   *to extinguish;*
                                to place outside
Gina has to remember to **put out** the fire that she
enjoys on cold nights.
The trash truck comes tomorrow; could you **put** the
garbage **out** for me?

stay up   *to remain awake, not to sleep*
Gina **stays up** to take care of her nightly routine.
On weekends I like to **stay up** and watch television.

Interview

The interviewer continues his conversation with
Gina.

Int: What's the next step in your routine?

Gina: Well, after brushing my teeth, I **take out**
        my pajamas and **put them on**. Then I **get
        into** bed.

Int: Do you generally sleep quickly?

Gina: No, it takes me some time to **doze off**.

Int: Do you watch television for a while?

Gina: Sometimes. I usually read a book or just
        look back on my day.

Int: Well, I'll leave now and let you start your
        routine.

Gina: Thanks. I'm **tired out** tonight. The
        sooner I can **go to bed**, the better!

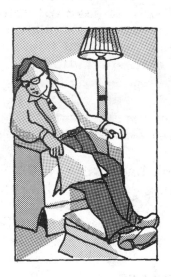

Expressions

be tired out	*to be very tired,* *to be exhausted*

Gina **is** too **tired out** to stay up and visit with the
interviewer anymore.
After working all day, Dr. Davis **was tired out** and
went straight to bed.

doze off   *to begin sleeping*
It takes Gina some time to **doze off** at night.
Listening to the radio helps me to **doze off** easily.

get into bed   *to lie under the sheets*
                        of a bed
After Gina puts on her pajamas, she **gets into bed**.
Be sure to take off your socks before you **get into
bed**.

go to bed   *to enter a bed*
The sooner Gina can **go to bed**, the better she will
feel.
Doris is sleepy during the day because she always
goes to bed late.

look back on   *to remember, to review*
Gina sometimes likes to lie in bed and **look back on**
the day she had.
As I **look back on** my life, I realize that I have made
many foolish mistakes.

take out   *to remove*
Gina usually **takes out** her pajamas after she brushes
her teeth.
Could you **take** the dishes **out** and set the table for
me?

EXERCISE 1

Select the correct idiom to complete each sentence.

1. You'd better _____ those tools before the children start playing with them.
   a. put away
   b. take out
   c. put out

2. As soon as the class _____, all the students rushed out of the room.
   a. let in
   b. looked back on
   c. came to an end

3. I had to use a fire extinguisher to _____ the small fire on my kitchen stove.
   a. take out
   b. put out
   c. doze off

4. If you're all _____ from a busy day, we can talk on the phone later.
   a. gone to bed
   b. gotten into bed
   c. tired out

5. Could you _____ the frozen meat and leave it on the kitchen counter?
   a. take out
   b. let in
   c. stay up

EXERCISE 2

**Fill in the blanks with the correct idiom. Each idiom is
used only once.**

look back on	staying up	at last
am tired out	take out	come to an end
doze off	put away	

A: _____this terrible day has ended. I
thought that it would never _____!

B: When I _____ this day, I want to forget
it completely. I really _____ from all that
hard work moving our belongings.

A: Me too. I don't want to _____ another
item from another box.

B: That's what happens when we move from one
apartment to another. I guess we won't be
_____ late tonight.

A: No, not at all. I want to lie down on the couch
and _____ for a while.

B: Sure. I'll _____ the rest of the clothes in
the closet.

Module 5 Review

EXERCISE 1

Select the correct idiom for the boldface phrase.

1. Kim **would prefer** to make sandwiches for lunch than eat out.
   a. sounds good
   b. takes her time to
   c. would rather

2. Don't **risk** getting hit by a car. Cross the street when the light has changed to green.
   a. take a chance of
   b. have your heart set on
   c. look forward to

3. It's more fun to **improvise** than to know what's going to happen in advance.
   a. play it by ear
   b. look back on
   c. have a ball

4. Bob offered to **pay the bill** for the group of us at the restaurant.
   a. live it up
   b. pick up the tab
   c. be broke

5. The door is locked and the children need to be **allowed to enter**.
   a. put away
   b. kept your eye on
   c. let in

6. On our last trip we travelled first class and really
   _____.
   a. lived it up
   b. stayed out
   c. stood up

7. The piano is too big for the room. It _____ too
   much space.
   a. puts on weight
   b. takes up
   c. puts out

8. I was so sleepy when I got home that I _____ on
   the couch.
   a. got in to bed
   b. stayed up
   c. dozed off

9. The police noticed that something was _____ in the
   store late at night.
   a. for nothing
   b. out of the ordinary
   c. nothing the matter

10. James really likes his office because it _____ a lake
    and garden.
    a. is nothing short of
    b. comes to an end
    c. looks out on

EXERCISE 2

Write a short story for each picture by using the suggested idioms. You may use other idioms as well.

1. (picture, page 131)
   let up, call off, would rather, take a chance

_____
_____
_____
_____
_____
_____

2. (bottom picture, page 132)
    take in, have one's heart set on, stay out,
    pick up the tab

_____
_____
_____
_____
_____

3. (right bottom picture, page 136)
    be tired out, stay up, get into bed, doze off

_____
_____
_____
_____
_____

4. (left top pictures, page 136)
    put out, put away, let in, at last

_____
_____
_____
_____
_____

Answer Key

Module 1, Lesson 1

Exercise 1

1.c, 2.b, 3.b, 4.a, 5.b

Exercise 2

day in and day out/wake up/goes off/pull themselves together/puts on/go over

Module 1, Lesson 2

Exercise 1

1.b, 2.c, 3.b, 4.c, 5.a

Exercise 2

get to/catch the bus/on time/makes good time/get on/get off

Module 1, Lesson 3

Exercise 1

1.a, 2.b, 3.c, 4.b, 5.a

Exercise 2

1. is in charge of
2. keep track of
3. in order
4. feel like
5. take some time off
6. on the other hand
7. right away
8. turn in
9. put up with

Module 1, Lesson 4

Exercise 1

1.b, 2.b, 3.a, 4.a, 5.c

Exercise 2

put...back/went for/got the most for/picked out/tried...on/make up my mind/think...over/changed your mind/bargain hunter

Module 1 Review

Exercise 1

1.a, 2.b, 3.c, 4.c, 5.b, 6.a, 7.a, 8.a, 9.c, 10.b

Module 2, Lesson 1

Exercise 1

1.c, 2.a, 3.b, 4.b, 5.c

Exercise 2

are free/am tied up/never mind/hear from/get in touch with/call...back/ make a call

Module 2, Lesson 2

Exercise 1

1.c, 2.b, 3.b, 4.c, 5.a

Exercise 2

look up/had to do with/filled out/fill in/looked over/putting together/went through/come in/by the way

Module 2, Lesson 3

Exercise 1

1.b, 2.a, 3.b, 4.c, 5.a

Exercise 2

first of all/far away/had better/shows up/before long/getting back

Module 2, Lesson 4

Exercise 1

1.b, 2.c, 3.b, 4.a, 5.c

Exercise 2

worked on/turned on/clued in/after a while/get the hang of/again and again/to their surprise/find out

143

Module 2 Review

Exercise 1

1.b, 2.a, 3.c, 4.a,   5.c
6.b, 7.a, 8.b, 9.c 10.a

Module 3, Lesson 1

Exercise 1

1.a, 2.b, 3.c, 4.b, 5.c

Exercise 2

giving me a hand/pitch in/am
used to/safe and sound/on
hand/just a minute

Module 3, Lesson 2

Exercise 1

1.a, 2.c, 3.b, 4.a, 5.c

Exercise 2

put forth/a number of/come
close to/work out/sit in on/on
and on/thought up/cut down on

Module 3, Lesson 3

Exercise 1

1.c, 2.c, 3.a, 4.c, 5.a

Exercise 2

all through with/play
catch/under the weather/coming
down with/take care of/took a
turn for the worse/something the
matter/pull up

Module 3, Lesson 4

Exercise 1

1.a, 2.b, 3.c, 4.a, 5.b

Exercise 2

going by/turn back/caught
fire/like crazy/runnin away/
toyed with the idea of/in a
moment/bringing back/turned
into/took guts

Module 3 Review

Exercise 1

1.b, 2.b, 3.a, 4.a,   5.c
6.c, 7.b, 8.c, 9.a, 10.b

Module 4, Lesson 1

Exercise 1

1.c, 2.c, 3.b, 4.a, 5.c

Exercise 2

go for a walk/take away/a little
way off/made friends
with/given...back/ count
on/grow up/through thick and
thin

Module 4, Lesson 2

Exercise 1
1.b, 2.c, 3.a, 4.a, 5.b

Exercise 2

in those days/believe in/fall in
love/going with/keep from/by
and by/drive away/make up/go
back/are all over

Module 4, Lesson 3

Exercise 1

1.c, 2.b, 3.a, 4.a, 5.c

Exercise 2

as a matter of fact/by
yourself/feel funny/new in
town/feel at home/ come from/is
on your mind

Module 4, Lesson 4

Exercise 1

1.b, 2.c, 3.a, 4.c, 5.c

Exercise 2

got off on the wrong foot/was
around/showing off/finding fault
with/putting up a front/look
down on/took advantage of/felt
sorry for

144

Module 4 Review

Exercise 1

1.a, 2.c, 3.b, 4.a, 5.c
6.c, 7.b, 8.a, 9.b, 10.a

Module 5, Lesson 1

Exercise 1

1.b, 2.a, 3.c, 4.a, 5.b

Exercise 2

looking forward to/was broke/go on a trip/turn up/once in a while/for free/on short notice/take up/out of the ordinary

Module 5, Lesson 2

Exercise 1

1.c, 2.b, 3.c, 4.a, 5.a

Exercise 2

on a diet/put on weight/nothing short of/nothing the matter/take your time/would rather/sound good

Module 5, Lesson 3

Exercise 1

1.a, 2,b, 3.c, 4.b, 5.a

Exercise 2

step out/let up/take a chance/kept our eye on/pigged out/call off/live it up/stayed out/had a ball

Module 5, Lesson 4

Exercise 1

1.a, 2.c, 3.b, 4.c 5.a

Exercise 2

at last/come to an end/look back on/am tired out/take out/staying up/doze off/put away

Module 5 Review

Exercise 1

1.c, 2.a, 3.a, 4.b 5.c
6.a, 7.b, 8.c, 9.b 10.c

Index

Note: The pages indicated are where the idioms first appear in this book.